351.2

Becoming a
FIREFIGHTER

LEARNINGEXPRESS®

NEW YORK

Copyright © 2008 LearningExpress, LLC.

All rights reserved under International and Pan-American Copyright Conventions.
Published in the United States by LearningExpress, LLC, New York.

Library of Congress Cataloging-in-Publication Data:
Becoming a firefighter.—1st ed.
    p. cm.
ISBN: 978-1-57685-655-0
    1. Fire extinction—Vocational guidance. I. LearningExpress (Organization)
TH9119.B43 2008
363.37023—dc22

                                                                2008021698

Printed in the United States of America

9 8 7 6 5 4 3 2 1

Regarding the Information in This Book
Every effort has been made to ensure the accuracy of directory information up until press
time. However, phone numbers and/or addresses are subject to change. Please contact the
respective organization for the most recent information.

For information on LearningExpress, other LearningExpress products, or bulk sales, please
write to us at:
  2 Rector Street
  26th Floor
  New York, NY 10006

Or visit our website at:
  www.learnatest.com

Contents

CONTENTS

Introduction

Why You Need This Book

THE NUMBER of paid, full-time firefighters in most parts of the United States—now at about 361,000—is expected to rise steadily through 2016. That's what the Bureau of Labor Statistics reports. That number doesn't include the estimated one million volunteer and on-call firefighters on whom many towns depend. Being a firefighter may be one of the most challenging jobs a person can have. Becoming a firefighter may be just as difficult.

Firefighting is a highly sought-after career. Because so many people want to work in the fire protection field, numerous candidates apply for each job opening. Expect stiff competition from these candidates. Although the minimum educational requirement in most cities and states is a high school diploma or GED (general equivalency diploma), anticipate that many of those competing with you for the same job(s) will have completed training courses. This advanced education includes certificate programs, which take weeks or months to complete, through college degrees, which require a commitment of a number of years.

You can increase your chances of being hired for a job in fire protection by reading this book and applying what you've learned to your job search. Not only will you learn about the various training courses available, but you'll see where to find them and how to pay for them as well. Other subjects covered include the complicated job application process, different types of jobs available in the field, and how to succeed once you've landed a job. Throughout the book, you will get helpful information from those already working in the field.

In Chapter 1, you'll get an inside look at the best opportunities in firefighting today, from municipal firefighter to fire inspector to federal, state, and private job possibilities. This chapter contains specific job descriptions, typical salaries, and minimum requirements for those jobs. We also cover trends in the education available to prospective and working firefighters. If you are willing to relocate to get the job you want, you'll find information about the fastest-growing fire departments in the country.

Chapter 2 shows you how to land a job in the fire service field. First, you'll read about the qualities possessed by the candidates who get hired. There is detailed information on every step of the application process for a range of positions, including how to prepare for the written and physical exams and how to ace oral interviews. No job search today is complete without the Internet, so we've provided tips for using it as well as many websites that can get your search started right away.

In Chapter 3, the education you'll need for your future career is explored, beginning with high school and the volunteer training available to teens. We'll explain the training courses offered beyond the high school level and provide actual degree requirements for fire science programs. These course descriptions can help you decide what training program is right for you and how long your schooling will last for each. You'll also find a directory of fire science training programs across the country in Appendix D.

After you've determined the education you need, Chapter 4 will explain the various ways with which to finance it. The general types of financial aid are explained, and the application process is broken down into easy-to-follow steps. You will even learn the largest sources of aid and where to look for more. Other helpful information includes glossaries of financial aid terms and acronyms.

Once you've completed your training program and landed your first job, Chapter 5 shows you how to succeed on that job. You'll be taken through the first days as a probationary firefighter through to advancement opportunities. The promotion process is explained, with job descriptions and sample job postings for advanced positions. Finally, you'll learn about other career options within the fire protection field.

Good luck with your job search and new career!

CHAPTER one

CHOOSING A CAREER IN FIREFIGHTING

THIS CHAPTER is a report on the current state of the firefighting field. You'll learn about the benefits of the job as well as emerging educational trends for prospective firefighters around the country. Job descriptions, requirements, and salaries are listed for the following entry-level positions: municipal and volunteer firefighters, state and federal wildland firefighters, military and private company firefighters, EMT (emergency medical technician) firefighters, fire inspectors, and fire protection engineers. The chapter ends with a quiz that may help you to find out if you're suited for this exciting career.

THE NATURE of firefighting has changed dramatically from the days when firefighters only responded to fires. Today, many firefighters are certified as EMTs or paramedics to meet the increasing need for such services. Many calls to the firehouse require emergency procedures unrelated to fires, such as providing help to a heart attack victim or dealing with hazardous materials. Firefighters also respond to terrorist attacks; earthquakes, hurricanes and other natural disasters; vehicle accidents, vehicle fires, and many miscellaneous 911 emergency calls. Therefore, firefighters need a broad range of skills, and they need to update their skills continually by receiving additional training. As new technologies and equipment are created and responses to emergencies and disasters change in scope, the demands on firefighters will become increasingly complex. However, along with all those demands come many benefits that firefighters receive while in the line of duty.

ADVANTAGES OF BECOMING A FIREFIGHTER

Men and women are attracted to the firefighting field for a variety of reasons. Some seek the adventure and excitement, while others like the stability of a profession with good benefits, a salary that increases with years of service, and a great retirement plan. Firefighters are also perceived well by the public, and many job candidates like the fact that, once hired, they will be looked upon as heroes. Let's look closely at some of the best aspects of the job.

Positive Public Perception

Although not all firefighters will admit it, most enjoy being perceived as heroes by the public. Many children look up to firefighters with awe and respect, often citing the profession as the one they want to enter when they grow up. Even among adults, firefighters are often treated with a great deal of respect because of the dangerous and heroic nature of their job. Not only do they save people's lives and property, but they also provide emergency assistance in natural disasters and other times of calamity.

The Tunnel to Towers Run

A run through an East River tunnel to the World Trade Center site is one of many honors for the 343 firefighters who died after the attacks on September 11, 2001. The run follows the route of Stephen Siller, a 34-year-old New York City firefighter, who ran in full gear through the tunnel to reach the towers in an effort to help. The father of five did not survive. Now, millions of dollars from the annual run goes to charities for children.

The Lure of Adventure

While firefighting is dangerous and demanding work, some people say they joined the profession because they enjoy the excitement and the rush of adrenaline that accompany fire calls. Each call can be different, and there is no way to predict the types of crises that will be met on each shift. Some firefighters jump out of airplanes to fight wildland fires, others scout out dangerous areas inside structures. Many firefighters save people's lives and property on a regular basis. They face danger and unknown conditions every time they go out on an emergency call.

Teamwork and Family Atmosphere

Firefighters live and work so closely with one another, so they often develop close bonds. Teamwork is essential in fighting fires and is emphasized from the start in all training programs. This teamwork provides a secure atmosphere for all the members of the team. Firefighters spend a great deal of time with each other when on long shifts at the firehouse; they often cook and eat large family-style meals around a big table and relax together when not out on calls. They take training courses together and test their skills by performing drills in friendly competition with each other. Kevin Scarbrough of the Ann Arbor, Michigan, fire department says firefighters sometimes play practical jokes on each other while in the firehouse to help relieve the buildup of tension from the underlying feeling of danger that accompanies most fire calls. The joking may also test how people will react to the group when in a fire situation.

Work Schedule

Firefighting is not a profession in which you'll end up behind a desk, working nine to five for five days a week. The variety of the work schedule appeals to people who want flexibility and large chunks of time off from work. Some firefighters even use their days off to earn side income, supplementing their firefighting salary. The average number of hours firefighters work each week is in the range of 42–52. Some of those hours, however, are spent in the firehouse, eating, sleeping, or relaxing.

In addition to waiting for calls, shifts involve firefighters engaging in a wide range of tasks, including maintenance of equipment and training, and may be followed by free time to relax. Schedules vary from department to department, but commonly firefighters work for 24 hours on duty followed by 48 or even

72 hours off duty. In large urban fire departments, each shift may be shorter, such as 8 to 14 hours, depending on if it is a day, night, or weekend shift.

Good Salary

The earnings of firefighters are high compared to other jobs requiring a similar amount of training. Typically, entry-level firefighters earn a significant salary, which then increases with experience and additional training. Most fire departments offer firefighters longevity pay after they've served a number of years. Longevity pay is a set amount added to firefighters' base salary every year after they become eligible to receive it. For instance, in the San Antonio, Texas, fire department, base pay increases by 3% for each five years of employment, up to 18% for 30 years.

Later in this chapter, you will find recent salary information for a number of jobs involving fire suppression and fire prevention. Many firefighters are also offered voluntary overtime on a rotating basis. Overtime offers a chance to increase your salary significantly, but it is an option that can also be rejected if the extra hours on the job aren't wanted. The only exception is when departments occasionally require mandatory overtime, such as in the case of a severe forest fire season.

Health, Life, and Disability Insurance Benefits

Firefighters usually have a choice of health plans (medical and dental) to select from their employer. These plans cover the firefighter and his or her dependents. Life and disability insurance are also provided. If firefighters are injured on the job, they can either get disability payments or retire early, depending on the nature of the injury and the department's guidelines. Indeed, most states require that all local fire departments offer disability retirement benefits to their firefighters.

Retirement Benefits

Firefighters normally receive excellent retirement benefits and retire earlier than those employed in other professions. Because of the arduous nature of the job, many firefighters retire as soon as they reach the eligible age or time on the job. For example, some firefighters need to work for 25 years or until they are 55 years old, whichever comes first. If you became a firefighter when you were 20 years old, you could retire at age 45. However, some departments require you to work until age 55, regardless of your age when you were hired (meaning that it is possible to retire, with benefits, after serving much less than 20 years).

As with many other jobs, firefighters can set aside a portion of their paycheck every month without paying tax on the money until they use it during retirement. This type of pension plan, often called a deferred compensation plan, also allows you to choose how the money is invested. Many fire departments will contribute to your pension plan, meaning that money you haven't earned or saved will be earning interest and waiting for you when you retire.

Access to a Union

Many firefighters belong to unions, either on a national or a local level. These unions represent the needs of their members by working for passage of laws and safety regulations, establishing training programs, and maintaining standards for the industry. The largest firefighter's labor organization in the country is the International Association of Fire Fighters (IAFF), which has more than 288,000 members. Some states have their own organizations. In California, the California State Firefighter's Association (CSFA) has been around for over 85 years and boasts more than 28,000 members. The CSFA uses its resources to negotiate better wages and benefits and fair personnel policies for its members. It also offers its members additional life, health, disability, group, and longterm care insurance.

JUST THE FACTS

The International Association of Fire Fighters is one of the oldest public employee unions in the country. It was formed in 1918, when firefighters were required to live in firehouses on 24-hour duty. There were very few civil service laws to protect public employees, so firefighters were at the mercy of local departments when it came to pay, promotions to better jobs, and benefits. The IAFF has worked to change those conditions, as well as to promote health and safety regulations for its members.

Miscellaneous Benefits

Other benefits commonly given to municipal firefighters include paid vacations, holidays, and sick time; a uniform allowance for laundry and purchase of new uniforms; free training programs and tuition assistance for college and university fire studies; sick leave accrual; a free annual medical examination; and physical-conditioning training and equipment to work on.

EDUCATIONAL TRENDS

While the published entrance requirements for becoming a municipal career firefighter are minimal, more and more applicants are gaining training and certification to boost their chances of getting hired. And fire departments are beginning to seek candidates who have continued their education beyond high school. As the demands on firefighters' skills increase, so does the demand for their education and training. For example, the Houston, Texas, fire department requires 60 hours of college credit with a grade "C" or higher, or two years of active duty military service. Years ago, firefighters could easily get hired with only the minimum requirements (having a high school diploma and being at least 18 years of age). However, in response to stiff competition for a limited number of jobs, serious applicants are now taking advantage of many training programs and coming to the job with at least some college credit.

Many prospective firefighters enroll in fire science certificate or associate degree programs or take specific courses such as Fire Hose and Fire Streams, Fire Behavior, Fire Tools and Equipment, and other fire-related courses to attain basic firefighting skills. Other prospective firefighters also complete associate in science (AS) degrees or obtain certificates from local colleges in Emergency Medical Technology (EMT) to increase their chances of landing a firefighting job.

To become the most attractive job candidate, you should consider education beyond high school. If you are in a medium to large city, chances are that some other applicants have or are attaining EMT, paramedic, or fire science training. Twenty-five years ago, when you were hired by a fire department, you were put through 12 to 16 weeks of training courses. Now, in cities like Miami, training takes six months. See Chapter 3 for more detailed information about the types of training programs that are available and how to choose the one that's best for you.

WHO EMPLOYS FIREFIGHTERS?

According to the Bureau of Labor Statistics, more than 361,000 career firefighters were employed nationwide as paid, full-time professionals in 2006 and employment is expected to continuously increase. Where are these career firefighters employed? Nine out of ten of them work for municipal or county fire departments, typically serving communities with populations of 50,000 or more. Not surprisingly, bigger cities are the largest employers.

Full-time firefighters are also hired by federal and state government agencies to protect government-owned property and special facilities. For example, the U.S. Forest Service, Bureau of Land Management, and Park Service offer both year-round and seasonal fire service jobs to protect the country's national parks, forests, and other lands.

In the private sector, many large industrial companies have their own firefighting forces, especially companies in the oil, chemical, aircraft, and aerospace industries. Other employers include airports, shipyards, and military bases. Also, a growing number of private companies are in the business of providing fire protection services, including on-call or on-site firefighting teams, to other businesses and institutions.

In addition to career firefighters, there are close to a million volunteer or paid-call firefighters nationwide. These individuals work mostly in rural or small communities and may receive compensation only when they are called to duty, or they may receive no monetary compensation at all but get free training and a uniform allowance.

FAST-GROWING GEOGRAPHIC LOCATIONS

You might consider relocating in your quest for a career firefighter position, because there are greater opportunities in some areas of the country than others. According to the Bureau of Labor Statistics, the states expected to increase their hiring of firefighters by 12% in the ten-year period from 2006 to 2016 include Utah, New Mexico, Idaho, and Arizona. Following close behind are Nevada, Florida, New Hampshire, Colorado, Alabama, and Washington state. Those employing the most firefighters and always looking for more include California, with a force of 26,810 in May 2007; Texas, with 26,210; and Illinois, with 16,940. When reading Chapter 2, keep in mind that the states whose forces are always growing are ones in which you might consider applying for a job.

WOMEN IN THE FIRE PROTECTION FIELD

The fire departments of many, if not most, cities are almost completely male. "We have a long way to go in making people aware that this is a job women are successful at. They love it and they want other young women to follow in their footsteps," Captain Brenda Berkman told an interviewer from the Associated Press. In 1982, Berkman was the first woman to become a New York City firefighter.

Berkman, who retired in 2006, filed a successful lawsuit against New York City in order to be hired. She said that the physical exam discriminated against women. Physical exams that test brute strength remain a stumbling block in many places. No one wants to reduce standards. But fire officials have suggested an exam that calls on candidates to show what they would actually do on the job, rather than simply demonstrate their strength. In Minneapolis, Minnesota, for example, women who pass the test are considered for the job, rather than just those with high scores.

Minnesota has been among the most successful states in recruiting, training, mentoring, and hiring female firefighters. At the time of a 2005 report, Minnesota had 95 women in eight departments. Seventeen percent served in Minneapolis. Other departments with relatively high percentages of women include Tacoma, WA; Madison, WI; San Francisco, CA; Boulder, CO; and Miami-Dade County, FL.

The first known woman firefighter in the United States was an African-American woman named Molly Williams. Williams was a slave, owned by a member of Oceanus Engine Company #11 in New York City. She was known to work in a calico dress and checked apron and was said to be "as good a fire laddie as many of the boys." During the blizzard of 1818, Williams distinguished herself by working in harsh conditions when male firefighters were scarce. Over the next hundred years, a handful of women worked as career or volunteer firefighters.

During World War II, large numbers of women began working in fire departments around the country to take the place of men who were serving in the military. The trend continued after the war, and in many cities all-women departments, paid and volunteer, were formed. In the beginning of the twenty-first century, there are an estimated 5,600 career women fire-fighters. They represent about 2% of the entire force, but their numbers are growing. In addition, there are an estimated 30,000 to 40,000 women vol-unteers and on-call firefighters. As they gain seniority and experience, women are being promoted in fire departments around the country.

JOB OPPORTUNITIES IN THE FIRE PROTECTION FIELD

Many people are needed to fight fires, both on the front lines and behind the scenes. While the majority of firefighters work for municipal fire departments, there are also jobs available in the private sector, the military, and state and federal governments. Several opportunities exist for volunteer firefighters in many locations across the country. In addition to these front-line positions, which deal mainly with actual fire suppression, there are other, less visible jobs in the firefighting field. These positions focus on fire prevention, and include fire protection engineers and fire inspectors. They make sure buildings and other sites are following safety codes; they can spot and correct fire hazards before a fire has a chance to start.

Following is more specific information on many of the entry-level job opportunities in the firefighting field. Keep in mind that job descriptions, minimum requirements, and typical salaries vary from position to position. As you consider your future career, you will need this information to help you decide which type of firefighting job best suits you.

Fire Suppression

As previously stated, the most visible jobs in the firefighting field involve fire suppression. These are the men and women who work to actively put out existing fires and offer assistance in emergency situations such as car accidents, terrorist activities, and hazardous material spills.

Municipal Firefighter

Nine out of ten firefighters work for municipal (local government) fire departments. Because this is the most common job in the firefighting field, it's the one about which you've probably heard the most. These are the firefighters who are paid, full-time workers (also called career firefighters, to distinguish them from volunteer or part-time firefighters). They fight fires and respond to emergency situations within their local community and may be called by surrounding fire departments to offer mutual aid for extremely serious fires.

Municipal firefighters work in teams and are assigned specific tasks to ensure optimal organization at the scene of a fire. Most fire departments have a combination of one or more of the following: engine company, ladder company, pump company, and truck company. Firefighters are assigned to one of these companies within the fire department, so they know exactly what they need to focus on when a fire call comes in. Some firefighters become apparatus operators (also known as fire truck drivers) after serving as firefighters for some time and passing a promotional exam; some are assigned pump duty; some enter burning structures to search for survivors; some handle the ladders while other firefighters are busy axing their way through the roof. Every fire call is different, but firefighters work together in an organized and systematic way by following the orders of their leader. He or she may be the fire chief, the assistant fire chief, the captain, or a person with some other title, depending on the size and location of the fire department.

There are several levels of rank for firefighters in municipal departments and many opportunities for promotion and advancement, depending on the size and location of the department. Most fire departments have a combination of the following job titles and ranks:

Firefighter Recruit	Battalion Chief
Firefighter Level I	District Chief
Firefighter Level II	Deputy Chief
Apparatus Operator (Truck Driver)	Assistant Fire Chief
Fire Lieutenant	Fire Chief
Fire Captain	

After completing the application process for a municipal firefighting position, applicants are rated and either placed on an eligibility list or eliminated from the process. If you are called from this list and you pass all subsequent tests and interviews and are hired, you move on to a training program. You'll be called a probationary firefighter (known as a *probie* to insiders) for the first 6 to 18 months, depending on the length of probation required in your area. See Chapter 5 for information about advancement opportunities within municipal fire departments.

Typical Minimum Requirements

While requirements vary, most municipal fire departments require applicants to have a high school diploma or GED, be at least 18 years old, and pass a physical ability exam. Some states require prospective firefighters to obtain state certification before being considered for a job. Because there is such intense competition for job openings, however, many applicants go well above the minimum requirements by getting volunteer firefighting experience and specialized training from a college fire science program to gain an edge on the competition.

Education beyond high school in other fields of study can also improve your chances of landing a job, as more and more departments are asking that candidates have some college credit. Chapter 3 has specific information about education, including fire science training programs. Other requirements may include no smoking, no drug use (you will be tested during the application process), and U.S. citizenship.

Typical Salaries

While income varies greatly depending on the location and availability of funds in each fire department, most firefighters earn a good salary, especially as they advance and attain higher levels of training. The following table shows firefighter salaries in a number of locations to give you an idea of what you can expect (figures are from the Labor Relations Information System; for the most recently compiled numbers, check out its website at www.lris.com). As stated earlier, if you find that your state comes in on the low end of the pay scale, you might want to consider relocating to an area of the country where firefighters are paid better. You can also find recent salary information in the annual publication, *Municipal Year Book*, in the reference department of your local public library.

What Entry-Level Firefighters Earn across the United States

Location	Monthly Wages
Anchorage, AK	$3,274
Los Angeles, CA	$3,781
West Hartford, CT	$3,790
Pensacola, FL	$1,854
Columbus, GA	$2,085
Terre Haute, IN	$2,695
Missoula, MT	$2,265
Cincinnati, OH	$2,462

According to *Fire Fighting News*, budget cutbacks have cost jobs in many fire-prone areas, especially in California. As it is, firefighters in the Forest Service may make up to $30,000 less than municipal firefighters.

Volunteer and Paid-Call Firefighter

It is estimated that of the more than one million firefighters in the United States, 815,500 are volunteers. Many prospective career firefighters first become volunteer firefighters in order to gain experience. Volunteering also allows them to use their skills as they conduct their job search or wait for their number to be called from eligibility lists of paid departments. Many volunteer fire departments require a large time commitment, and their firefighters receive little or no monetary compensation for their work. Volunteers are those who work for no pay, while paid-call firefighters usually receive minimum wage or a similar level of earnings for each fire call that they go on.

Volunteers may serve with career firefighters in the same fire company or they may comprise an entire fire company, with only a paid fire chief and assistant who work full time for the department. Some volunteer firefighters are given pagers, so they don't have to spend much time in the fire station waiting for calls. If they are on call and their pager goes off, they put a blue light/siren in the window of their car and drive to the fire station. There they get on the fire truck and head to the fire. Volunteer firefighters who are properly certified can perform the same functions that paid career firefighters do.

The experience you receive as a volunteer firefighter can be different, depending on the type of crew you work with. If you become a volunteer who works with a full crew of paid career firefighters, you can get an inside look at how things are run in the firehouse and at fires by a municipal department. This type of volunteer spends a specified number of hours at the firehouse instead of getting a pager and going on call. However, there may be some adjustment needed to fit in with the career firefighters when you are the only volunteer on duty. Some volunteers prefer a firefighting crew that is made up of all volunteers, to give them a feeling of camaraderie.

Typical Minimum Requirements

Requirements for volunteers have grown over the past 25 years. Although some counties and states still ask only that volunteers sign up and pass a physical exam, most demand extensive training. The typical training requirement includes a 100- to 150-hour course, plus another 75 to 100 hours of training if the department provides emergency medical care. Many volunteers are also given annual hazardous materials training, which ranges from 10 to 25 hours. In addition, they may be required to recertify their training every three to five years.

Jeffrey Cuttitta, a volunteer firefighter in Long Island, New York, said he went through several procedures before being selected to serve: a physical exam, ten weeks of classroom and ten weeks of hands-on training, a wait for an opening, and a swearing in. After joining the department, he became a probie. He then had to pass a written and a physical exam, attend all meetings and drills, and go to a predetermined number of fire calls for one year to get off of probationary status. Once the probationary period ended, Cuttitta went on to attain Firefighter I certification from the local fire academy.

Typical Salaries

While volunteers usually don't get paid, they enjoy several benefits: gaining firefighting experience, getting to know career firefighters, and learning to work as a team. Some volunteers do get small allowances to pay for their transportation to and from the fire department, and paid-call firefighters usually get minimum wage or a similar level of pay for each hour they spend on a fire call.

State Wildland Firefighter

Many state government agencies hire firefighters to protect state-owned land. Every year, these agencies have to deal with the threat of wildfires—fast-spreading burns that can scorch thousands of acres. These wildfires are often in remote regions with limited access, which makes fighting them perilous and brutal work. Fires on this scale are controlled not by using fire hoses, but by limiting where and how much the fire burns.

The states that employ the most firefighters are located in the western portion of the United States, because these states have the most forests or wildlands. However, other states also employ limited numbers of state firefighters. For example, in Minnesota, the Department of Natural Resources (DNR) has two divisions that hire seasonal firefighters: the forestry division and the state park division.

Most entry-level state firefighters are hired only during the season when most fires occur—and the fire season varies in each area of the country. Arizona, for instance, often employs firefighters from March to July (when monsoons arrive and fires are put out naturally) and then again in October if it is a dry year. California often doesn't hire until May, but its season can last until December.

Seasonal wildland firefighting differs from structural firefighting because of the nature and location of the fire. Much of the work is hard manual labor, such as cutting down brush and trees that are in the way of the fire. Excellent physical condition is required to keep up the pace of hard work for several days in a row as the fire rages. Most wildland fires last much longer than structural fires.

The California Department of Forestry calls itself the largest fire department in the country (at the state level), because it employs about 1,400 firefighters every fire season. The state posts its openings for firefighters each year, and on average more than 10,000 applications are received, meaning that there is great competition for these jobs. The filing deadline is usually in January or early February, and if you miss it, you must wait until the following year to sign up. Many states, though, such as those in the Southeast, often find themselves running short of personnel, particularly during the peak of the fire season.

Typical Minimum Requirements

Excellent physical condition is required for wildland firefighters because of the heavy manual labor, harsh conditions, longevity, and intensity of wildland fires. A good work record will increase your chances of getting hired, even if it is in an unrelated field. Because of the outdoor nature of the work, it is also advisable that applicants possess such skills as the ability to pitch a tent, cook over an open fire, and sharpen a knife. Knowledge of basic first aid and CPR (cardiopulmonary resuscitation) can also improve a candidate's chances of getting hired, as can proficiency with chain saws and trucks with 5-and-a-2 transmission. Every state requires that you be at least 18 years old and possess a high school diploma or its equivalent. There are additional requirements that vary from state to state, including having U.S. citizenship, not abusing alcohol or drugs, and passing a civil service exam.

Typical Salaries

The salaries are normally lower for entry-level state firefighters than they are for entry-level municipal firefighters, and the work is seasonal rather than year-round. The pay ranges from $8.30 to $10.00 per hour, but many firefighters get significantly more by adding overtime and hazard (actual frontline fighting) pay to their base pay. Also, firefighters who live in communities that have a high cost of living may receive higher wages.

Federal Wildland Firefighter

As with the state-level job just described, federal wildland firefighters fight fires in forests or wildlands. However, they are hired by the U.S. Department of the Interior and the U.S. Department of Agriculture and charged with protecting federal lands and parks rather than those maintained by individual states. The blazes these firefighters battle are caused by both human and natural forces, including, for example, the campfire that gets out of control and the bolt of lightning that hits dry brush. Like their state-level counterparts, federal firefighters also must engage in hard physical labor to stop raging forest or wildland fires.

For example, crews may be rushed into an area that is threatened, and told to scrape it down to mineral. This means that all the vegetation—dried grass, plants, dead wood, and anything else that would burn—has to be removed. This method of firefighting stops a fire by cutting back its fuel. In the wilds, this work may involve a four-person crew scraping an eight-foot-wide path for two miles. They must work fast, in hot, dry conditions, as the front of the fire approaches. Other tactics include starting and controlling a small fire and guiding it toward the front of the original fire to take away its fuel.

Large, raging wildland or forest fires can be like wars. Firefighting crews are flown and trucked in; air tankers are coordinated with the ground troops; support crews providing food, medical, and mail services converge on the scene. The shifts for firefighters can run 16 to 24 hours or more of hard physical labor in heavy gear as the air temperature often exceeds 100 degrees, which is why they need to be in excellent physical shape.

There are various levels and duties for federal firefighters. The first step is usually to work for a national forest, becoming a general wildland firefighter (referred to as a type-two firefighter) who works to support the frontline firefighting crew (called type-one firefighters). The next move up would be to join an engine company and work up to a type-one crew, the members of which are called hot shots and fight at the front line of the fire. Finally, you can apply to become a smoke jumper. Nationwide, there are currently about 2,200 firefighters who work as part of a hot-shot type-one team and about 400 smoke jumpers, with several thousand type-two firefighters. Timo Rivo, a smoke jumper who works out of Montana, explains the exciting role of a smoke jumper:

Smoke jumpers parachute out of airplanes to fight fires where no ground access is available. We carry heavy packs of supplies and stay out on the fire for up to three days before new provisions are dropped in to us or we leave the area. Sometimes we end up walking out after we conquer the fire and it might be a 16-mile trek back to the ground crew headquarters. Other times, we get a lift out on a helicopter, but overall, it is very demanding work. We need to pass grueling physical tests every year to maintain smoke jumper status.

Many federal firefighters are flown to different states to fight fires in a variety of locations throughout the fire season, depending on need and weather patterns. The agencies of the federal government that hire the most firefighters are the National Park Service, the Bureau of Land Management (both in the Department of the Interior), and the Forest Service (in the Department of Agriculture). See Appendix A for information on how to contact them.

Typical Minimum Requirements

Standards vary among the different branches of the federal government, but in general, applicants need to pass a physical agility test, be at least 18 years old, and have a high school diploma or its equivalent. The government ranks all of its jobs by grade, which also determines salary. The grade of the position(s) available is always included on a job listing and must be repeated on an application. In Chapter 2, you will find more detailed information on finding and applying for federal jobs.

For an entry-level position, at least three months of general work experience are also necessary. The government defines this as *any type of work that demonstrates your ability to perform the work of the position*. For a position above entry-level, work experience and education requirements increase. For a job at grade GS-5, you would need a year of specialized work experience (directly related to the job you are applying for), and a bachelor's degree with courses taken in a related field.

Typical Salaries

The salary for an entry-level federal firefighter starts at $8.59 per hour, but many firefighters get significantly more by adding overtime and hazard pay to their base. A move up to a position at grade GS-6 can entitle you to earn $15.42 to $20.04 per hour. The salaries for seasonal federal firefighters can vary greatly, depending on the length and severity of the fire season.

Military Firefighter

The U.S. Department of Defense also hires federal firefighters. Some may be deployed to combat zones. Others help in the protection of military bases. The bases employ enlisted men and women (and some civilians) to become base firefighters instead of relying on local municipal fire departments. The job duties of a military firefighter are basically similar to those of a municipal firefighter, so the job offers solid experience to someone who wants to apply for a municipal firefighting job after completing military service.

While all branches of the military employ firefighters, the Air Force and the Navy train and employ the most firefighters. The Air Force trains firefighters in how to protect aircraft when accidents occur during takeoffs and landings as well as how to fight structural fires and deal with hazardous materials. A 13-week fire academy training course, covering the basics of firefighting, is offered at the Goodfellow Air Force Base in San Angelo, Texas. The Air Force gives firefighters training on a regular basis, and their training courses offer students college credit from the Community College of the Air Force. Air Force firefighters can obtain an associate's degree through this ongoing training.

Most Air Force bases employ a mix of military members and civilians. Since military members are often moved around to different bases, depending on need, the civilian firefighters remain at the same base to maintain a sense of continuity. According to Floyd Virgil, a military firefighter at the Keesler Air Force Base, several of the civilian firefighters who work at the base were former military firefighters retired from active duty, so they came with experience when they applied for the job. He also states that military firefighters have a good chance of getting hired outside the military because it is well known that the military has excellent fire service training programs.

If this position interests you and you are not already enlisted in the Air Force, your first step is to contact a recruiter (listed in the yellow pages of your local phone book). In your initial meeting, ask the recruiter if you can get a guarantee of being trained and placed in the fire protection field. If you achieve a high enough score on the skills tests (the Armed Services Vocational Aptitude Battery, or ASVAB) and pass all other requirements, the Air Force may guarantee in writing that your career area will be within the fire protection field as a part of your enlistment agreement.

After you enlist, you will undergo six weeks of basic training at Lackland Air Force Base in San Antonio, Texas. If you have fire protection guaranteed as your career area, you will then be sent to the Goodfellow Air Force Base in San Angelo, Texas, for the 13-week training program before being assigned to a fire department. Air Force enlistment periods are for three to six years.

As with the Air Force, if you are not already enlisted, you must first contact a recruiter. This person will begin your application process by screening for minimum requirements and disqualifications. If the Navy accepts you, you will be sent for eight weeks and three days of basic training in Great Lakes, Illinois. You can choose to enlist in the Navy for a period of three, four, five, or six years.

The Navy's firefighters combat fires on its fleet of ships as well as other, related operations. This type of firefighting is often called damage control within the Navy. You can also check into getting a job with the aircraft fire rescue team in the Navy for aircraft that crash into the water. The Navy offers certified apprenticeship programs for some specialties within the firefighting occupation.

The increased visibility of firefighting in the Navy is evidenced by the Homer W. Carhart Award for Fire Protection Excellence. It was named after Dr. Homer W. Carhart, a Senior Scientist Emeritus at the Naval Research Laboratory (NRL) in Washington, DC, and an expert in the areas of safety, fire protection, and shipboard survivability. The award was established by the Chief of Naval Operations to recognize superior achievement in the areas of safety and shipboard survivability.

In 2004, HT 1 (SW) Christopher Regal received the award for his heroism aboard the ground-missile destroyer *USS Cole*. While on a refueling stop in Aden, Yemen, on October 12, 2000, the *Cole* was bombed by an explosive-laden boat that had pulled up alongside it. Right after the explosion, Regal helped rescue trapped sailors on the ship, which was badly damaged and filled with smoke. Several days later, Regal, exhausted and grieving for the 17 shipmates who had been killed, helped to save the ship, which had begun to sink.

Regal went on to become an instructor at the Naval Leadership Training Unit near Norfolk, Virginia. Events on the *Cole*, he told *Surface Warfare* magazine, "helped me refocus my goals, my expectations, and my skills. And for that, I think I got out of it more than I put in that day. I survived!"

Typical Minimum Requirements

The minimum requirements for all branches of the military are nearly identical. They require that their recruits

- ▶ be between 17 and 29 years of age
- ▶ be a U. S. citizen or have legal immigrant alien status
- ▶ have a clean arrest record
- ▶ be in good health and excellent physical condition
- ▶ pass a medical exam, including drug testing

To become a firefighter in the military, you also need to achieve an acceptable score on the ASVAB prior to enlisting. Applicants need to achieve a score of 90 in the general maintenance category to be admitted to the fire protection career area.

The 2000 Military Pay Chart

Basic Pay

Pay Grade	2 or less	Over 2	Over 3	Over 4	Over 6	Over 8	Over 10	Over 12	Over 14	Over 16	Over 18	Over 20
						Years of Service						
0-10												14,137.20
0-9												12,364.80
0-8	8,748.90	9,035.10	9,225.60	9,278.70	9,516.00	9,912.30	10,004.70	10,381.20	10,488.90	10,813.50	11,282.40	11,715.30
0-7	7,269.60	7,607.40	7,763.70	7,887.90	8,112.60	8,334.90	8,591.70	8,847.90	9,105.00	9,912.30	10,594.20	10,594.20
0-6	5,388.30	5,919.30	6,307.80	6,307.80	6,331.80	6,603.30	6,639.00	6,639.00	7,016.40	7,683.60	8,075.10	8,466.30
0-5	4,491.60	5,059.80	5,410.50	5,476.20	5,694.60	5,825.70	6,113.10	6,324.00	6,596.40	7,013.70	7,212.00	7,408.50
0-4	3,875.70	4,486.50	4,785.60	4,852.50	5,130.30	5,428.20	5,799.00	6,088.20	6,288.90	6,404.10	6,471.00	6,471.00
0-3	3,407.40	3,862.80	4,169.40	4,545.60	4,763.10	5,002.20	5,157.00	5,411.40	5,543.40	5,543.40	5,543.40	5,543.40
0-2	2,943.90	3,353.10	3,861.90	3,992.40	4,074.30	4,074.30	4,074.30	4,074.30	4,074.30	4,074.30	4,074.30	4,074.30
0-1	2,555.70	2,659.80	3,215.10	3,215.10	3,215.10	3,215.10	3,215.10	3,215.10	3,215.10	3,215.10	3,215.10	3,215.10
0-3				4,545.60	4,763.10	5,002.20	5,157.00	5,411.40	5,625.60	5,748.60	5,916.00	5,916.00
0-2				3,992.40	4,074.30	4,204.20	4,423.20	4,592.40	4,718.40	4,718.40	4,718.40	4,718.40
0-1				3,215.10	3,433.80	3,560.40	3,690.30	3,817.80	3,992.40	3,992.40	3,992.40	3,992.40
W-5												6,261.30
W-4	3,521.10	3,788.10	3,896.70	4,003.80	4,188.00	4,370.10	4,554.60	4,832.70	5,076.00	5,307.60	5,496.90	5,681.70
W-3	3,215.40	3,349.80	3,486.90	3,532.20	3,676.20	3,959.70	4,254.90	4,393.80	4,554.30	4,719.90	5,017.50	5,218.80
W-2	2,845.50	3,114.60	3,197.40	3,254.70	3,439.20	3,726.00	3,867.90	4,008.00	4,179.00	4,312.50	4,434.00	4,578.60
W-1	2,497.80	2,766.00	2,838.90	2,991.60	3,172.50	3,438.60	3,562.80	3,736.50	3,907.50	4,041.90	4,165.50	4,316.10
E-9							4,254.60	4,350.90	4,472.40	4,615.50	4,759.20	4,990.50
E-8						3,482.70	3,636.90	3,732.30	3,846.60	3,970.20	4,193.70	4,306.80
E-7	2,241.00	2,642.40	2,743.50	2,877.90	2,982.30	3,162.00	3,263.10	3,443.10	3,592.50	3,694.50	3,803.10	3,845.40
E-6	2,094.00	2,304.00	2,405.70	2,504.40	2,607.60	2,840.10	2,930.40	3,105.00	3,158.70	3,197.70	3,243.30	3,243.30
E-5	1,918.80	2,047.20	2,145.90	2,247.30	2,405.10	2,570.70	2,705.40	2,722.20	2,722.20	2,722.20	2,722.20	2,722.20
E-4	1,758.90	1,848.90	1,949.10	2,047.80	2,135.10	2,135.10	2,135.10	2,135.10	2,135.10	2,135.10	2,135.10	2,135.10
E-3	1,587.90	1,687.80	1,789.80	1,789.80	1,789.80	1,789.80	1,789.80	1,789.80	1,789.80	1,789.80	1,789.80	1,789.80
E-2	1,509.90	1,509.90	1,509.90	1,509.90	1,509.90	1,509.90	1,509.90	1,509.90	1,509.90	1,509.90	1,509.90	1,509.90
E-1	1,347.00	0.00										

Source: www.dfas.mil/militarypay/militarypaytables.html

Key to Military Ranks

Army Ranks

E-1: Recruit
E-2: Private
E-3: Private First Class
E-4: Corporal/Specialist
E-5: Sergeant
E-6: Staff Sergeant
E-7: Sergeant First Class
E-8: Master Sergeant
E-9: Sergeant Major

Navy Ranks

E-1: Airman or Seaman or Fireman or Construction Recruit
E-2: Airman or Seaman or Fireman or Construction Apprentice
E-3: Airman or Seaman or Fireman or Construction
E-4: Petty Officer Third Class
E-5: Petty Officer Second Class
E-6: Petty Officer First Class
E-7: Chief Petty Officer
E-8: Senior Chief Petty Officer
E-9: Master Chief Petty Officer

Air Force Ranks

E-1: Airman Basic
E-2: Airman
E-3: Airman First Class
E-4: Senior Airman
E-5: Staff Sergeant
E-6: Technical Sergeant
E-7: Master Sergeant
E-8: Senior Master Sergeant
E-9: Chief Master Sergeant

Marine Ranks

E-1: Private
E-2: Private First Class
E-3: Lance Corporal
E-4: Corporal
E-5: Sergeant
E-6: Staff Sergeant
E-7: Gunnery Sergeant
E-8: Master Sergeant or First Sergeant
E-9: Master Gunnery Sergeant or Sergeant Major

Coast Guard Ranks

E-1: Recruit
E-2: Fireman or Seaman Apprentice
E-3: Fireman or Seaman
E-4: Petty Officer Third Class
E-5: Petty Officer Second Class
E-6: Petty Officer First Class
E-7: Chief Petty Officer
E-8: Senior Chief Petty Officer

Typical Salaries

Salaries for firefighters in the military are calculated in the same way as those for other military jobs. They may be found on the military base pay chart, found on page 20, which takes rank and years of service into account. The dollar amounts in the table combine basic pay, basic allowance for quarters, basic allowance for subsistence, and the average variable housing allowance. They also include the tax advantage from untaxed allowances. The figures do not include the average overseas housing allowance or the overseas cost-of-living allowance.

Firefighters in Private Companies

In addition to the many job opportunities offered by government agencies, there are firefighting jobs available with private companies. You can look for jobs from the following types of businesses:

- oil and chemical refineries
- large corporations
- airports
- shipyards

A majority of private-sector jobs for firefighters can be found with companies in the petrochemical, aircraft, and aerospace industries such as Boeing. Many private firefighters become highly specialized by focusing their training and inspection activities on one location and the major threat in that area, such as oil fires at an oil company or airplane fires in an airport.

There is a growing trend for private firefighting companies to set up shop to provide firefighters to various companies, sometimes along with additional fire prevention and protection services. One such company is Rural/Metro Corporation, which currently provides fire protection services to more than 400 communities and responds to more than 1 million calls annually. It is based in Arizona but has offices across the nation. You may find job opportunities with private companies by searching the Internet. Try using search terms such as *firefighting* and *employment* or *fire suppression* and *jobs*.

Typical Minimum Requirements

The minimum requirements for each private company vary. In general, as with most firefighting positions, applicants should be in good physical condition and have solid work experience to get the best opportunities for fire-fighting jobs in the private sector. Some specialized training, such as having hazardous materials certification when applying to oil and chemical companies, could also prove beneficial. Many private firefighting companies have a selection process similar to that of municipal fire departments, and require thorough written and physical testing and some form of fire service training before hiring applicants.

Typical Salaries

Salaries vary among the different private fire companies, just as they do in other private industries. However, most companies will have salaries similar to that of municipal firefighting departments, in order to recruit high-quality applicants.

EMT Firefighter

Firefighter EMTs or paramedics are trained to provide emergency medical care, including ambulance services. They respond to a variety of emergency situations as well as fires. For example, they assist victims of natural disasters and spills of hazardous materials as well as medical emergencies, such as heart attacks, strokes, and choking. They assess, manage, and administer treatment to ill or injured persons on the way to hospitals or other medical facilities, most often in a life-support unit or an ambulance. EMTs rely on radio communication to transmit information about a patient's condition and to receive medical instruction from a physician or other medical professional. The level of treatment they are allowed to provide depends upon their level of training and certification.

Three levels of EMT certification are recognized by the National Registry of Emergency Medical Technicians: Basic, Intermediate, and Paramedic. Training programs are offered nationwide from colleges and universities; hospitals; and police, fire, and government health departments. Most EMT-Basic programs are modeled on a 110-hour standard training course developed by the U.S. Department of Transportation. Candidates must meet certain minimum requirements (for example, a minimum age of 18, high school diploma or GED, and valid driver's license). Programs for EMT-Intermediate and EMT-Paramedic cover progressively more advanced levels of medical treatment and require completion of the prior level(s) of training.

Some fire departments, such as that of Seattle, Washington, now require all new firefighter hires to become certified as an EMT-Basic or an EMT-Paramedic on a routine basis instead of allowing firefighters to choose to specialize in this area. Large urban departments in particular look for or require EMT training, because of their high level of responsibility for providing emergency medical services in the community.

Typical Minimum Requirements

To acquire EMT-Basic certification, you need to complete an approved training program, usually consisting of approximately 100 to 120 hours of study. EMT-Intermediate certification requires approximately 35 to 55 hours of instruction in addition to EMT-Basic training. EMT-Paramedic is the most advanced level of EMT training and requires approximately 750 to 2,000 hours of training in total (including the EMT-Basic and EMT-Intermediate hours of training). EMT-Paramedics often complete an associate in science degree in the course of their training.

Typical Salaries

EMT firefighters earn salaries above those of firefighters without EMT training. Here are some examples of base annual salaries for EMT firefighters in cities around the country.

Anchorage, Alaska	$54,803
Lexington, Massachusetts	$43,830
Kennedale, Texas	$40,532
Gladstone, Missouri	$34,295–$36,031
Upland, California	$52,896–$64,296
Margate, Florida	$42,988
Phoenix, Arizona	$40,475–$47,475
Forest Park, Georgia	$35,040
Washington, DC	$48,731

Fire Prevention

We have covered the most popular positions in the area of fire suppression, which involves the act of physically fighting fires. But the firefighting field is also made up of those who work to prevent fires. Fire inspectors and fire prevention engineers help to protect the public by making our structures and vehicles safer before and after they are built and by educating us about fire safety and fire prevention.

Fire Inspector

Most fire inspectors' work involves commercial or other nonresidential structures. They examine these buildings to eliminate fire hazards and to monitor fire protection equipment, such as sprinkler systems, extinguishers, and alarms, to ensure operability. Inspectors also patrol industrial sites to determine whether hazardous and combustible materials are stored properly. According to Kevin Scarbrough, an experienced fire inspector in Ann Arbor, Michigan, many inspectors focus on the construction of new buildings to ensure that they meet all required state and local fire codes as they are being built. Some also offer fire education information to schools and local civic groups.

The job of fire inspector is held both by those trained in fire inspection procedures and by experienced firefighters who took promotions and gained additional training to land the position, depending on the organizational structure and size of the fire department. Historically, the fire inspector was a firefighter first and then learned the duties of fire inspection through promotional exams. The growing trend now is for fire departments or fire prevention bureaus to hire entry-level fire inspectors who have specialized college-level training but no firefighting experience.

Typical Minimum Requirements
Depending on the fire agency doing the hiring, requirements vary greatly. You must have a high school diploma and at least four years of experience in the field. In some fire departments, you have to serve as a firefighter for several years (anywhere from 4 to 15 years or more) to be eligible for promotion to inspector. Other fire departments open up the position of fire inspector to graduates of fire science degree programs who have never served as firefighters. Skills that most departments look for are the abilities to lead the work of others, perform many complicated tasks, and plan and accomplish goals.

Typical Salaries
Salaries vary among departments and locations, but the median for 2008 was $49,537. This figure includes salaries for both entry-level fire inspectors and long-term firefighters promoted to inspector. For those who have been firefighters for several years before being promoted, the salary range is high relative to that for entry-level fire inspectors. In Philadelphia, for example, fire inspectors may earn $74,930.

Fire Protection Engineer
Some experts estimate that for every graduate going into fire protection engineering, five job openings await. The need for qualified fire protection

engineers is so high that many companies actively recruit on college campuses where fire engineers receive their training. Fire protection engineers take advanced courses in mathematics, physics, and chemistry to gain scientific knowledge used in the research, design, installation, and operation of physical systems related to fire safety. They often work outside of fire departments, usually in the private sector. The majority of fire protection engineers do not begin their careers as firefighters.

Fire protection engineers are often called upon to provide a broad range of services. Some perform fire safety evaluations of building and industrial complexes to determine the risks of fire loss and to find the best ways to prevent fires. Others design systems that automatically detect and suppress fires and explosions as well as fire alarm, smoke control, emergency lighting, communication, and exit systems. Fire protection engineers perform research on materials and consumer products or on computer modeling of fire and smoke behavior. Some investigate fires or explosions and prepare technical reports or provide expert courtroom testimony in civil litigation cases.

Many fire protection engineers are hired to oversee the design and operation of safety procedures for large companies. This is an area of major concern to complex manufacturing facilities, such as refineries, chemical plants, and multinational business networks. These companies know that a million dollars spent on prevention and preparation can save tens of millions in cleanup costs and fines, not to mention the invaluable savings in terms of presenting a good image to the public.

Fire protection engineers also work for insurance companies, surveying major facilities and performing research, testing, and analysis. As the computer and electronics industry grows, its special fire prevention needs expand as well. When a room full of high-tech gear is threatened by fire, the best course of action usually is not to turn on water sprinklers. Finding new ways to prevent and suppress fires and save costly equipment is proving to be a viable new avenue for employment.

Architectural and engineering firms, automatic sprinkler companies, large hotel chains, and specialty consulting groups also hire fire protection engineers. Besides in private-sector companies, fire protection engineers work at all levels of government around the world. Other interesting careers in the field include those in trade associations, in testing laboratories, and at colleges and universities.

Typical Minimum Requirements

Fire protection engineers need a more advanced educational background than firefighters do. The engineers' training typically includes a bachelor of science (BS) degree in a traditional engineering field or in fire science and often a master's degree (MA) in fire protection. If you are in high school and considering this career, consult Chapter 3 for information on the colleges and universities that offer the program you need. Start preparing early by taking and doing well in math and science classes.

Typical Salaries

They usually attain a higher level of education than career firefighters. (Fewer than 5% have doctorates.) And their services are greatly in demand. As a result, fire protection engineers usually earn more money—more than the average salary for a conventional engineer.

The mean salary for an entry-level fire protection engineer is $55,000 a year. A master's degree takes that figure up to $65,000. After being in the job from six to eight years, a fire protection engineer can earn a median salary of $72,500. A master's degree can help a midlevel fire protection engineer earn close to $100,000.

Senior level fire protection engineers—those who've been on the job 15 years or longer—can earn more than $120,000 a year. In addition to the usual benefits, fire protection engineers sometimes get to travel to other parts of the world, where their skills are in as great demand as they are at home.

Want to Know More?

For more information about becoming a fire protection engineer, the Society of Fire Protection Engineers (SFPE) may be a helpful group to contact. Request a free copy of the SFPE Guide to Careers in Fire Protection Engineering. Write to the society at 7315 Wisconsin Avenue, Suite 620E, Bethesda, MD 20814. You can also visit the group's career website at www.careersinfireprotectionengineering.com.

IS FIREFIGHTING THE RIGHT CAREER FOR YOU?

You have read the job descriptions for a variety of fire-related positions, and perhaps you find more than one appealing. To discover which position might best suit you, take the following test. It is designed to help you determine whether a career in firefighting or fire prevention is right for you, allowing you to see the traits that fit each field best. Write down your yes or no answers to the following questions and then take a look at what those answers mean by consulting the explanation at the end of the test.

1. Are you physically fit and do you have good upper-body strength?
2. Do you enjoy working out and staying in shape?
3. Do you enjoy working in teams?
4. Do you like to get adrenaline rushes?
5. Do you prefer a flexible work schedule?
6. Do you enjoy enforcing rules?
7. Do you like to teach others?
8. Do you smoke cigarettes or cigars?
9. Do you enjoy a daily routine that is similar every day?
10. Do you value a high level of privacy and space at work?
11. Can you follow instructions properly and quickly?
12. Do you enjoy working outdoors?
13. Are you interested in learning about medical emergency technology?
14. Are you flexible and adaptable?
15. Can you think on your feet in situations of chaos and stress?
16. Do you prefer a regular work schedule that is the same every week?
17. Is working out and staying in shape a constant battle for you?
18. Are you afraid of heights or closed-in spaces?
19. Do you have a strong sense of independence?
20. Would you enjoy studying chemistry and physics?
21. Can you handle seeing gory and unpleasant things at work?
22. Are you willing to risk your life to save others?
23. Do you enjoy the thrill of adventure?
24. Do you enjoy experiencing new situations each day?
25. Do you like to play team sports?

If you answered yes to the majority of questions numbered 1 to 5, 11 to 15, and 21 to 25, then you should consider a job in fire suppression. If you answered yes to the majority of questions numbered 6 to 10, and 16 to 20, then you may prefer a job in fire prevention or other fire-related services, rather than fire suppression. If you answered yes to all of the questions, you are well suited for a career in either fire suppression or fire prevention/instruction. However, if you answered no to the majority of the questions, you may want to reconsider your future in the firefighting field.

INSIDE TRACK

Wayne Williams
Smoke Jumper Foreman
U.S. Forest Service

I started working for the California Division of Forestry back in 1974 when I was 18 years old, and I started with the Forest Service in 1975. I worked on a wildland firefighting truck in the Eldorado National Forest outside of Lake Tahoe and started as a smoke jumper in 1977. I've been a smoke jumper since then.

I really like the job a lot—I don't really have any dislikes about it. I feel fortunate to have had this career, and I'll be retiring . . . when I'm 50 with full benefits. I feel lucky. Also I think that structural firefighters have a much more difficult and dangerous job—as wildland firefighters, smoke jumpers don't have to contend with the hazards of working inside of a burning structure.

I work year-round, five days a week, but the schedules vary—when we're on a fire we may be working 16 to 18 hours a day. We get one mandatory day off every 14 days. Smoke jumpers are unique in that when we're not working a fire, a lot of our time is spent making our equipment—we're all trained in how to manufacture our own parachutes, packs, jumpsuits, and other pieces of equipment.

I think that the job of a smoke jumper has definitely changed for the better since I began. It's much safer, mostly due to technology and training. In addition to the rookie training, every spring we go through a refresher course that lasts for about two weeks.

The main advice I'd give to someone who wants to be a smoke jumper for the Forest Service is to start getting wildland firefighting experience as soon as possible. Technically, you need a couple of seasons of this experience, but in reality the competition may have as many as ten seasons, so you have to get as much as you can. Start out small, with local and state agencies, and start making your way up the ladder.

CHAPTER two

APPLYING FOR THE JOB

THIS CHAPTER gives you the information you need to apply for and land a job as a firefighter in any of the following areas: municipal fire department, state or federal government, the military, or a private fire company. For municipal fire departments, which hire the most firefighters annually, you'll get tips on how to succeed in every portion of the formal application process: the written exam, the physical ability test, the oral interview, the oral board, and much more. You'll get the latest information on how you can use the Internet to land a job as well as how veteran's preference points can boost your application's score.

AS YOU'VE learned, competition for firefighting jobs is stiff. When you find an opening and apply for a position, you will most likely be one of many applicants competing for the same job. Most fire departments put job applicants through a rigorous selection process that can take from several months to a year or more, because they want to find firefighters who will excel on the job. Firefighters need to be smart enough to learn the chemistry, physics, and biology of emergency services; strong enough to carry a person out of a burning building; fit enough to respond to several emergencies in a day, sometimes without sleep; honest enough to be trusted inside every home and business in town; and compassionate and polite enough to interact with the public daily.

What can you do to edge out the competition? The first step is to understand what fire departments are looking for in the candidates they hire. Make sure you have done all you can to make yourself the best job candidate you can be. Then arm yourself with the latest information on the application process. If you know what to expect, you'll be ahead of the competition, who may fail one or more steps in the process simply because they didn't know what was expected.

THE CANDIDATE FIRE DEPARTMENTS WANT TO HIRE

The application process is designed to weed out those who don't have what it takes to work in the fire protection industry and to seek out those who do. While there are many very different steps in the process, they all have that same goal. Generally speaking, fire departments are looking for applicants who

▶ have the education required (the minimum is a high school diploma or GED)
▶ are stable and secure, with the ability to handle stress
▶ conduct themselves appropriately (traffic tickets, misdemeanor charges, drug use, or a poor work record can take an otherwise good candidate out of the running)
▶ are in excellent physical condition
▶ do not smoke (not required by all departments, but the requirement is on the rise)
▶ have experience (with a Fire Explorer program, or a volunteer department)
▶ are certified to perform CPR and/or have training as an EMT or paramedic
▶ have certification (required by some states) from a fire science training program
▶ have acquired more than the minimum required education (by taking college courses or getting a degree in fire science management, hazardous materials, and/or fire protection engineering)

Fire departments can learn about many of the items in this list by having the prospective firefighter fill out an application and send in documents such as school transcripts. Other criteria are more subjective, and hiring departments use a number of techniques to find suitable applicants. The possible steps in the application process for municipal firefighters follow later in this chapter. Not all of the hiring process steps described are required by every fire department. You can look up the specific requirements for several locations in one of the books mentioned in Appendix C under the heading *Test Prep Materials*.

Additional Possible Requirements

Some fire departments may also require

▶ testing: drug screening, psychological examination, medical examination, background investigation (which may include checking your personal references, criminal and driving records, and fingerprints), and a polygraph (lie detector) test

▶ proof of residency, voter registration certificate, proof of citizenship (birth certificate, naturalization papers, or baptismal papers), and a valid driver's license

▶ uncorrected vision of at least 20/50 in both eyes; some fire departments require 20/20; others have no uncorrected limits

▶ certification that you have not smoked a cigarette, cigar, or pipe in the past year

PLAN FOR SUCCESS

Now that you have an idea of what is expected of you, you can formulate a plan for success. Whether you are about to enter the field or are still in school with a few years before you begin a job search, there are things you can do right now to get ready for your career in fire protection:

▶ do well in school and get your diploma

▶ begin a lifelong habit of staying in good physical condition

▶ stay out of trouble: drinking, drug use, vandalism, stealing, and other illegal behavior could make it hard or impossible for you to have the career of your choice

▶ do your best at your current job: show up on time; treat your boss, coworkers, and the public with respect; build a reputation you'll be proud to talk about with your future employer

- ▶ consider enrolling in a Fire Explorer program
- ▶ get involved in your community by volunteering
- ▶ if you are in high school, consider college and/or military service

JUST THE FACTS

Fire Prevention Week is held every year during the week around October 9, in commemoration of the Great Chicago Fire of 1871. The fire, which resulted in 250 deaths and millions of dollars worth of damage, led to the practice of fire prevention rather than simply firefighting.

MUNICIPAL FIREFIGHTER SELECTION PROCESS

The application process for the position of municipal firefighter includes many steps that are also found in the processes for state, federal, and private firefighting company jobs. The steps will be explained in detail only in this section. The selection process goes far beyond merely filling out the application forms, although those application forms can be long and unwieldy. This section will lead you through the entire application process, giving you tips and techniques for doing your best and for increasing your chances of getting hired at the end of the process. By reading this section, you can find out how to make the most of each step of the application process before you begin. That way, you can stay a step ahead of the competition.

The Exam or Position Announcement

Applying to be a firefighter differs from applying for most other jobs. The differences begin with the exam or position announcement. You rarely see fire department openings advertised in the Help Wanted section of the newspaper. Instead, the city usually starts looking for potential firefighters by means of a special announcement. This announcement will outline the basic qualifications for the position as well as the steps you will have to go through in the selection process. It often tells you some of the duties you will be expected to perform. It may give the date and place of the written exam, which is usually the first step in the selection process.

To get a copy of this announcement, check your public library. You may also get one directly from the fire department or city personnel department. If exams are held irregularly, the fire or personnel department may maintain a mailing list so that applicants can receive an exam announcement the next time an exam is scheduled. If exams are held frequently, you will sometimes simply be told to show up at the exam site on a given day of the week or month. In those cases, you usually get more information about the job and the selection process when you pass the written exam. Study the exam announcement as well as any other material, such as brochures, that the department sends you.

What Is an Eligibility List?

Most fire departments or the city personnel departments that handle the selection process for them establish a list of eligible candidates, ranking them from highest to lowest. This is commonly referred to as the eligibility list. How ranks are determined varies from place to place. Sometimes the rank is based solely on the written exam score, sometimes on the physical ability test, and sometimes on a combination of factors. Even if you make it through the entire selection process, the likelihood that you will be hired as a firefighter often depends on your placement on this list, which is determined by the quality of your performance in one or more parts of the selection process.

Make a commitment now: You need to work hard, in advance, to do well on the written exam, the physical ability test, and the oral interview (if there is one), so that your name will stand out at the top of your agency's eligibility list. You should aim to get 100% correct answers on every test to get a chance at coming out toward the top of the list. Some applicants may be getting extra points for living in the jurisdiction or for active military duty, so you need to score very high to compete with them. Often firefighters on waiting lists will have scores of 100 to 105 on account of extra points, so don't plan on merely passing with a score in the 70s or 80s if you want to get called from the eligibility list.

The Application

Often the first step in the process of becoming a firefighter is filling out an application. It may be a form on which you provide information about your education, employment experience, and personal data; or it may be an application to take the written or the physical test, with the more complete form coming later in the process. In any case, at some point you will probably be asked some questions you wouldn't expect to see on a regular job application. You might be asked things like whether you've ever gotten any speeding tickets or been in trouble with the law, whether you've used illegal drugs, or even whether any relatives work for the city or the fire department. Your answers to these as well as the more conventional questions will serve as the starting point if the department conducts an investigation of your background, so it's important to answer all questions accurately and honestly.

Application Tips

- Print your answers, or write as legibly as you can.
- Neatness and accuracy count. For example, filling in your apartment number in the blank labeled *city* reflects poorly on your ability to follow directions.
- Verify all information you put on the form. Don't guess or estimate; if you're not sure of the exact address of your high school or what year you worked for a certain company, look it up.
- If you're mailing your application, take care to submit it to the proper address; it might go to the personnel department rather than to the fire department, so follow directions.
- Make a copy of your application before sending it in, so you can use it as a guide when filling out additional applications.

Sample Applications

The sample applications on the following pages gives you an idea of what you might be filling out as an initial step in becoming a firefighter. These applications are provided as samples only; they cannot be used to submit to any fire departments. You need to get an original application form from the appropriate department when you're ready to apply. However, you can read through these samples to find out what sort of information you'll be asked to provide and to practice filling out the application. Don't underestimate this step. Filling out the application neatly and accurately can make or break your quest for employment, because it is a key part of the employment process.

City of Cincinnati
Department of Personnel
Two Centennial Plaza, Suite 200
805 Central Avenue
Cincinnati, OH 45202

An Equal Opportunity Employer

Open to the Public
Application for

_____

Title of position

First Name:	Middle Initial:	Last Name:

Apartment or Box #: Street Address:	Soc. Sec. No.:

City:	State:	Zip:

Day Phone:	Evening Phone:

CIRCLE ONE

Are you at least 18 years of age?	Yes	No
Have you worked for the City of Cincinnati in the last 2 years?	Yes	No
Do you have a valid driver's license? (Show to staff or mail a copy.)	Yes	No
Do you have a professional license or certificate or CDL? (If so, attach a copy.)	Yes	No
Do you request 5 points for being an honorably discharged veteran? (If so, attach a copy of DD 214)	Yes	No
Do you request 10 points for having a service-connected disability of 10% or more? (If so, attach a copy of DD214 and official statement from the Veteran's Administration.)	Yes	No
Have you ever been convicted of any traffic violations or paid any tickets?	Yes	No
Have you ever been convicted of any other local, state, or federal offense?	Yes	No
May we contact your present employer without contacting you first?	Yes	No
Do you request any reasonable accommodation? (If so, attach a Request for Reasonable Accommodation Form.)	Yes	No

Place a check by each item that you have attached to your application.

Copy of Driver's License (if application is mailed)		Work Experience Form(s)	
Reasonable Accommodation Request		Copy of Transcript(s)	
Copy of license or certificate or CDL		Resume	
Other:		Applicant Flow Sheet	
Copy of statement from Veteran's Administration		Copy of DD214	

All information provided by me in support of my application for employment is true and correct to the best of my knowledge. I understand that misrepresentations or omissions may be cause for rejection, or may be cause for subsequent dismissal if I am hired. I hereby authorize any present or former employer, person, firm, corporation or government agency to answer any and all questions and to release or provide any information within their knowledge records. I agree to hold any and all of them blameless and free of any liability for releasing any truthful information that is within their knowledge or records.

Signature: _____ Date: _____

INITIALS OF PERSONNEL DEPARTMENT STAFF ONLY: DRIVER'S LICENSE SHOWN   YES_____ NO_____
CDL SHOWN   YES_____ NO_____

Department of Human Resources
24-Hour Job Information Hotlines:
Open Competitive: (800) 970-5478
Transfers/Promotional Opportunities for curr
County employees: (213) 974-8335
TTY: (800) 899-4099   http://dhr.lacounty.ir

Please Read Carefully

1. COMPLETING YOUR APPLICATION:

a. THE APPLICATION SHOULD BE COMPLETE AND ACCURATE BEFORE SIGNING. INCOMPLETE APPLICATIONS CANNOT BE ACCEPTED.

b. Your SOCIAL SECURITY NUMBER MUST BE INCLUDED for record control purposes. Federal law requires that all employed persons have a Social Security Number.

c. To receive APPROPRIATE CREDIT, include a copy of your diploma, transcript, certificate, or license as directed on the bulletin.

2. MINIMUM OR SELECTION REQUIREMENTS are listed in the examination bulletin.

a. YOUR APPLICATION WILL BE ACCEPTED ONLY IF IT CLEARLY SHOWS YOU MEET THE REQUIREMENTS. The information you provide will determine your eligibility and is subject to verification at any time.

b. You must be at least 16 years of age at the time of appointment unless other age limits are stated on the bulletin. The Federal Age Discrimination in Employment Act (ADEA) of 1967, as amended, prohibits discrimination on the basis of age for any individual over age 40.

c. Your experience may be paid or unpaid unless the bulletin states otherwise. Report it as "volunteer" or "unpaid" in the box for monthly salary. Experience is evaluated on the basis of a verifiable 40-hour week.

3. APPLICATION DEADLINE:

a. If the bulletin has a closing date, submit the application and all required information as listed on the bulletin by the specified deadline. POSTMARKS WILL NOT BE ACCEPTED. **LATE APPLICATIONS WILL NOT BE ACCEPTED.**

b. Applications for positions designated "**Apply in Person**" must be filed in person at the address given. Filing may be closed without notice.

4. PROMOTIONAL EXAMINATIONS:

a. Please list separately the PAYROLL TITLE for each job. Do not group your experience. If more space is needed, attach additional sheet(s) to your application. Specify the beginning and ending dates for each job. If you have been promoted, do NOT list all of your time with the County under your present payroll title.

b. Some of your experience may have been in a position in which such work is not typically performed. If such experience is permitted as indicated in the examination bulletin, it will not be considered unless it is verified in writing by your department's Human Resources Office. A signed Verification of Experience letter must be filed with your application or submitted by the last day for filing, or it will not be accepted.

c. Permanent employees who have COMPLETED THEIR INITIAL PROBATIONARY PERIOD AND HOLD A QUALIFYING PAYROLL TITLE may file for promotional examinations if they are within six months of meeting the experience requirements by the last day of filing or as otherwise indicated on the bulletin.

5. VETERANS PREFERENCE CREDIT of 10 points will be added to your final passing grade in any open competitive examination if you are an honorably discharged veteran who served in the Armed Forces of the United States:

a. During a declared war; or

b. During the period April 28, 1952 through July 1, 1955; or

c. For more than 180 consecutive days, other than for training, any part of which occurred after January 31, 1955, and before October 15, 1976; or

d. In a campaign or expedition for which a campaign medal or expeditionary medal has been authorized and awarded.

This also applies to the spouse of such person who, while engaged in such service was wounded, disabled or crippled and thereby permanently prevented from engaging in any remunerative occupation, and also to the widow or widower of any such person who died or was killed while in such service. A DD214, Certificate of Discharge or Separation from Active Duty, or other official documents issued by the branch of service are required as verification of eligibility for Veterans Preference Credit. If you are unable to provide any documentation at the time of filing, the 10 points will be withheld until such time as it is provided.

6. CHANGE OF NAME OR ADDRESS should be reported in writing immediately to the department to which you submitted your application. Include your Social Security Number, former name and/or address, as well as your new name and/or address and the title(s) and number(s) of the examination(s) for which you have applied.

7. EQUAL EMPLOYMENT OPPORTUNITY/NON-DISCRIMINATION POLICY:

a. It is the policy of the County of Los Angeles to provide equal employment opportunity for all qualified persons, regardless of race, color, religion, sex, national origin, age, sexual orientation or disability.

b. If you require material in an ALTERNATE FORMAT or are an individual requesting REASONABLE ACCOMMODATION(S) in the examination process for a physical or mental disability, please CONTACT THE AMERICANS WITH DISABILITIES ACT (ADA) COORDINATOR LISTED ON THE EXAMINATION BULLETIN. The provision of reasonable accommodation may be subject to verification of disability as allowable with State and Federal law. All disability-related information will remain confidential.

8. RECORD OF CONVICTIONS: A full disclosure of all convictions is required. Failure to disclose convictions will result in disqualification. Not all convictions constitute an automatic bar to employment. Factors such as your age at the time of the offense(s), and the recency of offense(s) will be taken into account, as well as the relationship between the offense(s) and the job(s) for which you apply. However, any applicant for County employment who has been convicted of workers' compensation fraud is automatically barred from employment with the County of Los Angeles (County Code Section 5.12.110). **ANY CONVICTIONS OR COURT RECORDS WHICH ARE EXEMPTED BY A VALID COURT ORDER DO NOT HAVE TO BE INCLUDED.**

County of Los Angeles
EMPLOYMENT APPLICATION

Department of Human Resources
24-Hour Job Information Hotlines:
Open Competitive: (800) 970-5478
Transfers/Promotional Opportunities: (213) 974-8335
TTY: (800) 899-4099   http://dhr.lacounty.info

Please Print

Last

First

Middle

1a. EXAM NUMBER	1b. EXAMINATION TITLE		**OFFICIAL USE ONLY**	☐ ACCEPTED	☐ DENIED

2. SOCIAL SECURITY NUMBER (needed for record control purposes)	Analyst	Date

3. NAME	Last	First	M.I.	

OTHER NAMES USED IN EMPLOYMENT	Last	First	M.I.

4. ADDRESS	Number	Street	Apt. #

City	State	Zip

5a. HOME PHONE ( )	5b. BUSINESS/MESSAGE PHONE ( )	Final Score	Group	Veterans Credit	Withhold Date

5c. E-MAIL ADDRESS

6. Please check all areas in which you would accept employment. You will be considered only for areas checked.

A. ☐ **Any Area** (If you check this box, no need to check any other area boxes.)

B. ☐ **Antelope Valley** Palmdale/Lancaster

C. ☐ **San Fernando Valley** Burbank/Glendale/Northridge/Santa Clarita

D. ☐ **San Gabriel Valley** Pasadena/Monterey Park/El Monte/Pomona

E. ☐ **Metro** Los Angeles/West Hollywood/Eagle Rock

F. ☐ **West** Malibu/Santa Monica/Beverly Hills

G. ☐ **South** Inglewood/ Compton /Willowbrook/Watts

H. ☐ **East** Montebello/ Downey /South Gate/Whittier

I. ☐ **South Bay/Harbor** Carson/Torrance/Long Beach/Hermosa Beach

7. Indicate the type of appointment you will accept:
A. ☐ Full-time Permanent (40 hours per week)   B. ☐ Temporary   C. ☐ Recurrent, As Needed, or Seasonal

8. Shifts you are willing to work:
A. ☐ Day   B. ☐ Evening   C. ☐ Night   D. ☐ Rotating   E. ☐ On Call   F. ☐ Weekend   G. ☐ Any

9. Do you know any language other than English?   ☐ YES ☐ NO   If YES indicate language(s):
A _____   B _____   C _____
☐ Read ☐ Speak ☐ Write   ☐ Read ☐ Speak ☐ Write   ☐ Read ☐ Speak ☐ Write

10. Have you ever been a County of Los Angeles employee?   ☐ YES ☐ NO   If "YES," please complete the following information.

Employee Number	Payroll Title		Item Number	Employment Status: ☐ Permanent
Department			Department Number	☐ Temporary ☐ Recurrent

11. If a license or certificate (including Bilingual Certificate) is required for this job, list those you possess and provide dates of expiration.

License or Certificate	Number	Date Issued	Expiration Date

12. To qualify for employment you must be either (a) a citizen of the United States of America, or (b) a registered alien with government permission to work in this country. Does either statement (a) or (b) describe your status as a resident of this country?   ☐ YES   ☐ NO

13. Do you claim Veterans Credit? (Veterans Credit is applicable to open competitive examinations only.)   ☐ YES   ☐ NO
If "YES," attach a copy of your DD214, Certificate of Discharge or Separation from Active Duty, or other official documents issued by the branch of service. (See Application form Information Sheet for Veterans Credit criteria.)

14. Have you ever been fired or asked to resign?   ☐ YES ☐ NO
If "YES," please attach an explanation with the name and address of the company, and the date and the reason for the termination.

15. Have you ever been convicted of a misdemeanor or felony by a criminal or military court?   ☐ YES ☐ NO
If "YES," please complete the Record of Convictions section below.
List all convictions. **Attach an additional sheet if necessary.**

NAME (Please Print)	Last	First		M.I.
OTHER NAMES USED				
SOCIAL SECURITY NUMBER		DATE OF BIRTH	Month	Day	Year
OFFENSE or CASE NAME (Give Penal or other code section if known)			CASE NUMBER	
CONVICTION/ORDER DATE	Month	Day	Year	LOCATION OF COURT	City		State
SENTENCE or FINE				

Revised November 2004

EDUCATION: High School Graduate? ☐ YES ☐ NO If "NO," number of years completed in High School _____ GED Certificate ☐ YES ☐ NO

Show courses you have completed that are required and others directly related to the job for which you are applying. In order to receive CREDIT FOR COLLEGE WORK, be sure to include a copy of your diploma, transcript, or certificate unless otherwise directed by the job bulletin.

NAME AND LOCATION OF COLLEGES OR SCHOOLS ATTENDED	DATES ATTENDED	CREDITS COMPLETED		MAJOR SUBJECT OR COURSE	UNITS COMPLETED IN MAJOR	DEGREES OR CERTIFICATES RECEIVED
		SEMESTER	QUARTER			
	FROM					
	TO					
	FROM					
	TO					
	FROM					
	TO					

REQUIRED OR RELATED COURSES: (Attach an additional sheet if necessary to list all courses completed)

SCHOOL	COURSE NAME	UNITS	SCHOOL	COURSE NAME	UNITS

WORK EXPERIENCE: Beginning with your most recent experience, please account for all employment and any periods of unemployment in the last ten years. Include self-employment, military service, and volunteer work related to the job for which you are applying. Also list any jobs held more than ten years ago which relate to the duties of the job for which you are applying. Please list separately the PAYROLL TITLE of each job in which you have been employed. Describe the work you did as completely as possible and list each job separately. If you need additional space to describe your duties, you may attach a resume or additional documents to further describe your qualifications unless otherwise directed by the job bulletin. All the requested information MUST be completed.

PRESENT/LAST EMPLOYER or COUNTY DEPARTMENT	PAYROLL TITLE (for each title use a separate section)	NUMBER YOU SUPERVISED
EMPLOYER'S ADDRESS	DUTIES	
CITY/STATE ZIP CODE		
FROM Month Day Year TO Month Day Year TOTAL MOS. WORKED		
HOURS PER WEEK SALARY HOURLY ☐ MONTHLY ☐	REASON FOR LEAVING	Are you employed by this company now? ☐ YES ☐ NO If "YES," may we contact your employer? ☐ YES ☐ NO

EMPLOYER or COUNTY DEPARTMENT	PAYROLL TITLE (for each title use a separate section)	NUMBER YOU SUPERVISED
EMPLOYER'S ADDRESS	DUTIES	
CITY/STATE ZIP CODE		
FROM Month Day Year TO Month Day Year TOTAL MOS. WORKED		
HOURS PER WEEK SALARY HOURLY ☐ MONTHLY ☐	REASON FOR LEAVING	

EMPLOYER or COUNTY DEPARTMENT	PAYROLL TITLE (for each title use a separate section)	NUMBER YOU SUPERVISED
EMPLOYER'S ADDRESS	DUTIES	
CITY/STATE ZIP CODE		
FROM Month Day Year TO Month Day Year TOTAL MOS. WORKED		
HOURS PER WEEK SALARY HOURLY ☐ MONTHLY ☐	REASON FOR LEAVING	

Certification of Applicant: I certify that all statements made in this application and on any attachments included are true and complete to the best of my knowledge. I understand that any false statement(s) of material facts or omissions may subject me to disqualification or dismissal.

Print Name _____ Signature _____ Date _____

COUNTY OF LOS ANGELES

How did you learn about this position?

A. ☐ Ad   B. ☐ County Employee   C. ☐ County Bulletin Board   D. ☐ Campus Recruitment   E. ☐ Library

F. ☐ Job Fair   G. ☐ Internet   H. ☐ Job Hotline   I. ☐ Other

----

EQUAL EMPLOYMENT OPPORTUNITY QUESTIONNAIRE

Exam Number: _____ Exam Title: _____

The following voluntary information is requested for the County of Los Angeles to evaluate its hiring practices and to prepare repor required by law for the State and Federal Government. This form will be detached from the employment application. This information w be confidential and will **NOT** be used to make a decision about your employment.

A. Please mark the group that best describes your race/ethnicity.			B. Gender
1. __ White	3. __ Black/African American (not of Hispanic origin)	5. __ Hispanic/Latino (Mexican, Puerto Rican, Cuban, Central or South American, or other Spanish culture or origin, regardless of race)	☐ Female ☐ Male
6. __ American Indian (subject to verification)	7. __ Asian or Pacific Islander (excluding Filipino)	8. __ Filipino	

DATE OF BIRTH Month Day Year	NAME Last First M.I.

☐ Disabled – A person with a disability is an individual who: (1) has a physical or mental impairment or medical condition that limits one or more life activities, such as walking, speaking, breathing, performing manual tasks, seeing, hearing, learning, caring for oneself or working; (2) has a record or history of such impairment or medical condition; (3) is regarded as having such an impairment or medical condition.

The Written Exam

In most jurisdictions, taking a written exam is the next step in the application process. The written exam is your first opportunity to show that you have what it takes to become a firefighter. As such, it's extremely important. People who don't pass the written exam don't go any farther in the selection process. Furthermore, the written exam score often figures into an applicant's rank on the eligibility list. In some cases, this score by itself determines your rank, while in others it is combined with other scores, such as physical ability or oral board scores. The exam bulletin may specify what your rank will be based on.

Written exams for most municipal fire departments test basic skills and aptitudes: how well you understand what you read, your ability to follow directions, your judgment and reasoning skills, your ability to read and understand maps and floor plans, your math skills, and sometimes your memory. In this type of preliminary written exam, you will not be tested on your knowledge of fire behavior, firefighting procedures, or any other specific body of knowledge. This test is designed only to see if you can read, reason, and do basic math.

In some places, taking the exam involves studying written materials in advance and then answering questions about them on the exam. These written materials generally have to do with fire and firefighting, but all you have to do is study the guide you're given. You're still being tested just on your reading skills and memory, and there are good reasons for this. Firefighters have to be able to read, understand, and act on complex written materials, not only fire law and fire procedures, but also scientific materials about fire, combustible materials, chemicals, and so forth. See the sidebar on the opposite page for what an experienced firefighter from Dallas, Texas, has to say.

Indeed, firefighters have to be able to think clearly and independently, because lives depend on decisions they make in a split second. They have to be able to do enough math to read and understand pressure gauges or estimate the height of a building and the amount of hose needed to reach to the third floor. They have to be able to read maps so they can get to the emergency site quickly, and floor plans, so they can find their way to an exit, even in a smoke-filled building.

Some people think that all you need is physical strength and a hefty dose of courage to become a good firefighter. That is a typical misconception that the public often has about what it takes to become a firefighter. In reality, we have to know a lot about fire and smoke and how they are affected by a building's construction. We have to know how fire travels, what will make it larger, what parts of buildings are the most dangerous, and a lot of other scientific things. In order to gain the necessary knowledge, we undergo training programs on a regular basis. If you don't have basic math, reading, and reasoning skills, you won't be able to cut it as a firefighter.

Most exams are multiple-choice tests of the sort you've often encountered in school. You get an exam book and an answer sheet on which you have to fill in circles or squares with a number two pencil. Try the following practice test to familiarize yourself with this format and with the types of questions you will likely be asked.

Applicants are generally notified in writing about their performance on the exam. The notification may simply say whether or not you passed, or it may tell you what your score was. It may also say when you should show up for the next step in the process, which is often the physical ability test.

Written Exam Tips

- Ask for and use any material the fire department or personnel department publishes about the written test; some agencies have study guides, and some even conduct study sessions.
- Locate and read test-preparation books geared for firefighting written exams, to increase your score (see Appendix C for a list of useful test preparation books).
- Prepare by taking many practice tests.
- Try to find people who have taken the exam recently and ask them about what was on the exam. Their hindsight—"I wish I had studied . . ."—can be your foresight.

Practice Test

This practice test contains questions similar to those you might see on an actual test. It should give you a sense of what you might expect to find on a written exam, but it should not be used to assess whether you are prepared for your actual exam. It only offers a sampling of each question type; it does not include every possible question type. You might also find map-reading, mechanical aptitude, charts and graphs, and other such questions on a written exam. For more test preparation materials, see Appendix C.

Questions about You

These are questions that ask your responses to various situations. In some cases, you may think that different responses are true of you in different situations. You still need to choose the response that seems most like you, most of the time.

These questions are to help us understand you. It is better to be honest about how you would handle a situation than to try to guess how you *should* handle it. If you try to predict what the right answer is supposed to be, you may often be wrong. In addition, you may present an unrealistic, misleading, or inconsistent picture of yourself.

1. When you are talking to someone who has recently been involved in a dangerous situation, such as a car accident, it is better to
   a. get the person to focus on the facts of what happened, rather than talking about his or her feelings.
   b. allow the person to talk about his or her feelings while describing what happened.
2. When a coworker is having personal problems that are affecting his or her ability to get the job done, it is better to
   a. encourage the person to tell you about the problems so that you can help.
   b. let the coworker know that you would be willing to take some of his or her work if it would help.
   c. not discuss personal problems at work and let the person work them out for him- or herself.
   d. encourage the coworker to talk to someone who can help him or her solve those personal problems.
3. When you make decisions, you prefer to
   a. make a decision by yourself, then get input from others before you take action.
   b. consider your options, then get input from others before you decide.

    c. formulate some ideas to present to others, then let the group decide.

    d. discuss your ideas with others to develop options before you decide.

4. After someone has explained something new to you, such as during training for a new job, you usually

    a. are able to remember all the information you need.

    b. remember most of what you were told.

    c. wish you had listened better when it was being explained.

Reading Comprehension

Questions 5 to 8 refer to the following reading passage:

The emotional abilities children acquire in later life build on those of the earliest years, and these abilities are the essential foundation for all learning. Successful learning is not predicted by how many facts a person knows or the ability to read so much as by emotional and social measures: being self-assured and interested; knowing what kind of behavior is expected and how to rein in the impulse to behave poorly; being able to wait, to follow directions, and to turn to others for help; and expressing needs while getting along with others.

A child's emotional abilities depend on the most basic of all knowledge, how to learn. There are seven key ingredients of this crucial capacity, all related to emotional intelligence:

Confidence. A sense of control and mastery of one's body, behavior, and world; the child's sense that he or she is more likely than not to succeed at what he or she undertakes and that adults will be helpful.

Curiosity. The sense that finding out about things is positive and leads to pleasure.

Intentionality. The wish and capacity to have an impact and to act upon that with persistence. This is related to a sense of competence, of being effective.

Self-Control. The ability to modulate and control one's own actions in age-appropriate ways; a sense of inner control.

Relatedness. The ability to engage with others based on the sense of being understood by and understanding others.

Capacity to Communicate. The wish and ability to exchange ideas, feelings, and concepts verbally with others. This is related to a sense of trust in others and pleasure in engaging with others, including adults.

Cooperativeness. The ability to balance one's own needs with those of others in group activity.

5. According to this passage, which of the following is true?

   a. The ability to read is not important to a child's successful learning.

   b. A child's level of emotional intelligence is highly related to how well the child can control his or her impulses.

   c. Emotional intelligence is learned early in life and does not change once adulthood is reached.

   d. A child's level of emotional intelligence is independent of the child's ability to learn in school.

6. Sara is selling chocolate bars to raise money for the school's new gymnasium. The first ten people she asks refuse to buy any chocolate. According to this passage, she should

   a. think of other ways to make money for the new gymnasium instead of continuing to fail.

   b. stop trying to sell the chocolate since she has been unsuccessful.

   c. freely vent her frustration to other students who are selling more candy.

   d. believe that she will begin to sell more chocolate, if she remains positive and keeps trying.

7. A class is attending a science fair at which there are several new scientific inventions. As the children walk past the displays, one of the students, Joseph, talks to the other students about topics not related to the science fair. When he is not talking, he is watching all the people around him. Based on the information in this passage, what do you think about Joseph's behavior?

   a. He is balancing his need to socialize with the need to let other students enjoy the science fair.

   b. He is lacking self-control, because he does not like the science fair.

   c. He seems to lack a natural curiosity and appreciation for learning about new things.

   d. He feels understood only if he is talking about himself.

8. A school counselor notices that a young student named Marisha is a loner. She speaks only when someone speaks to her first. During lunch and in classes, she sits by herself. Which of the seven key ingredients for being able to learn does Marisha seem to be missing?

   a. confidence

   b. curiosity

    c. intentionality

    d. self-control

    e. relatedness

    f. capacity to communicate

    g. cooperativeness

Writing Skills

The writing skills section of the test may have questions similar to any of the following. The format of the questions will vary.

In the examples, numbered 1 to 4, there are several writing errors. You will find one of these types of errors in each of the questions numbered 9 to 14.

Examples:

1. Grammar Error Example:

    Incorrect: The woman has went to the store.

    Correct: The woman has gone to the store.

2. Punctuation Error Example:

    Incorrect: After reading the book you will write a report.

    Correct: After reading the book, you will write a report.

3. Capitalization Error Example:

    Incorrect: You should turn left on Main street.

    Correct: You should turn left on Main Street.

4. Spelling Error Example:

    Incorrect: The two women went into businiss together.

    Correct: The two women went into business together.

Questions 9 to 14. For each question, identify the type of error (as in example 1 to 4), and mark that number on your answer sheet.

9. It is a well-known fact that everyone experiences dreams during sleep. The value and importence of

10. dreams, however—has been debated over the centuries. Nevertheless, many people would like to

11. remember their dreams, but have difficulty doing so. Since many dreams ocur shortly before a person

12. awakes, you can often "Catch" yourself dreaming by setting your alarm for 15 minutes before you normally

13. get up. Your dreams may provide interesting insights into your life. As psychologist Carl Jung has wrote,

14. "The dream is the small hidden door in the deepest, and most intimate sanctum of the soul."

15. Choose the statement below that you think is the most clear, concise, and effective. It should also contain correct grammar, punctuation, and spelling.

   a. A White House Commission have recommended a number of steps, to improve air safety, including fingerprinting all airline employees.

   b. A White House commission recommended a number of steps to improve air safety, one of which would be to fingerprint all Airline Employees.

   c. A White House Commission recommended a number of steps, such as fingerprinting all airline employees to improve Air Safety.

   d. A White House commission has recommended a number of steps to improve air safety, including FBI checks of fingerprints of all airline employees.

In the following question, fill in the blank with the correct word or phrase.

16. Joe, Bill, and __ decided to go to the meeting together.

   a. us

   b. me

   c. I

   d. them

Mathematical Skills

You will not be allowed to use a calculator on the test.

17. What is the decimal equivalent of $\frac{6}{15}$?

   a. .25

   b. .30

   c. .35

   d. .40

18. A piece of rope is 50 feet in length. It is found that the rope shrank by 10% when it got wet. After drying, the rope was stretched 5% longer than its wet length. How long is the rope after it is stretched?

   a. 57.50 feet

   b. 55.00 feet

   c. 47.50 feet

   d. 47.25 feet

Situational Questions

These questions measure a variety of skills, including problem solving, decision making, and judgment, as well as many other relevant skills. Try to place yourself in each situation, or remember a situation you have been in that was similar to the one described, and choose the response (or responses) that you think best. If none of the answers is exactly what you would do or what you think would be best, choose the answer (or answers) that comes closest to how you feel or think.

19. Lately you have noticed an increase in salespeople coming to your door trying to sell you various items. You find this irritating, and you wish they would stop. What is the best way to solve this problem? Choose two answers.

    a. Let the salespeople tell you about their products before deciding whether you are interested.

    b. Politely tell each salesperson that you are not interested in buying anything.

    c. Angrily tell each salesperson to leave you alone.

    d. Refuse to open your door to anyone who looks like a salesperson.

    e. Put up a sign on your door that says "No Solicitors."

    f. Let the salespeople believe that they are close to making a sale, then tell them to leave.

20. You are attending a playoff game for your university basketball team, the Tigers. They are playing the Elks. As you go to get a hot dog, you accidentally bump into an Elks fan. Even though you apologize, he turns to you and yells: "What's the matter with you, you idiot? You better look where you're going, you stupid Tiger fan. Where'd you get that stupid hat? All you stupid Tiger fans are wearing those stupid hats. Those hats are stupid and you're stupid!" You do not feel threatened by the man, but you think he is irritating. Of the following, which would you be most likely to say? Choose three answers.

    a. "You're the one who's acting stupid here."

    b. "Excuse me. I'm going back to my seat now."

    c. "Like I said, I'm sorry I bumped into you."

    d. "Move away from me please."

    e. "I'm just here to have fun at the game."

    f. "Security can kick you out of here for bothering people."

    g. "Why don't we just go back to our seats and enjoy the game."

    h. "Hey man, let's forget the insults."

    i. "No wonder everyone thinks Elks fans are a bunch of hotheads."

21. You are going to move out of a house after renting it for three years. The house is in good condition. When the landlord inspects the house, he says that you will have to paint the inside of the house or he will keep your security deposit. You have called the local housing authority and have found out that painting is your landlord's responsibility. When you tell him this, he still disagrees. What do you do?

   a. Do the painting yourself, and insist on getting your deposit back.

   b. Tell him that you will pursue the matter legally.

   c. Offer to pay for half of the painting if he will give you your deposit back.

   d. Give up on getting your deposit back, because it is not worth the fight.

Answers to the Practice Test

Questions about You

Questions 1 to 4 ask you to answer honestly how you would respond in these situations. Therefore, there is no right answer. Your honest answers allow the fire department to learn about who you are, one of the important purposes of the written exam.

Reading Comprehension

5. **b** is correct because self-control is one of the emotional skills listed in the passage.

6. **d** is correct. Sara is demonstrating intentionality by believing that she can sell more chocolate.

7. **c** is correct. Based on Joseph's behavior, it is not clear if any of the other statements are true.

8. **f** is correct. Marisha clearly has trouble communicating with others. She may also lack confidence or relatedness, but we can't tell that for sure from her behavior.

Writing Skills

9. **4** is correct. The word *importance* is misspelled.

10. **2** is correct. The punctuation of *however—has* is incorrect. The correct punctuation is *however, has*.

11. **4** is correct. The word *occur* is misspelled.

12. **3** is correct. The word *catch* should not be capitalized.

13. **1** is correct. "Jung wrote," is correct, not "has wrote."

14. **2** is correct. There should not be a comma between *deepest* and *and most*.

15. **d** is correct. The other options all have at least one punctuation or capitalization error. In addition, choice **d** provides the information in the most concise yet complete way.

16. **c** is correct.

Mathematical Skills

17. **d** is correct. To solve this problem, divide 6 by 15.

18. **d** is correct. To solve this problem, first multiply 50 by .10. This is equal to 5. Next, subtract 5 from 50. The result is 45. Then multiply 45 by .05. This is equal to 2.25. Lastly, add 2.25 to 45.

Situational Questions

19. **b** and **e** are the best choices. Did you remember to choose two answers?

20. **b**, **c**, and **g** are the best choices. Did you choose three answers?

21. **b** is the best choice. In this case, the landlord is breaking the law. Telling him your intention gives him the opportunity to change his mind.

The Physical Ability Test

The physical ability test is the next step in the process for many fire departments. You may be asked to bring a note from your doctor saying that you are in good enough shape to undertake the physical ability test before you will be allowed to participate. This is probably an indication that you should expect the test to be tough. Firefighting is, after all, physically demanding work. Lives depend on whether your strength, stamina, and overall fitness allow you to carry out the necessary tasks during an emergency. If you make it to the academy and later into a fire company, you can expect to continue physical training and exercises throughout your career. In fact, some cities require all firefighters to retake the physical ability test every year.

The exact events that make up the physical ability test vary from place to place, but the tasks you have to perform are almost always job related; they're a lot like the physical tasks you will actually have to perform as a firefighter. Many times the test is set up like an obstacle course, and is timed, with a cutoff time for passing. Often you have to wear full, heavy protective gear, including an air pack, throughout these events. Here's an example of the events in a test that you would typically have five to seven minutes to complete:

▶ dummy drag
▶ hose drag

▶ stair climb

▶ tunnel climb

▶ ladder raise and climb

▶ wall jump

In an obstacle course setup like this one, you might be given the opportunity to walk the course before you actually have to take the test. Take advantage of the walk-through. In departments where the physical ability test figures into your rank on the eligibility list, merely meeting the maximum time to pass isn't good enough; people who have faster times will be higher on the list than you are. You can usually find out just what tasks are included in the physical ability test from the exam announcement or related materials.

Different departments have varying policies on retesting if you fail. Some allow you to retest on the same day after a rest period. Some allow you to come back another time and try again, usually up to a set maximum number of tries. In some departments, your first try is the only chance you get; if you fail, you're out, at least until the next testing period. Not many departments will allow you to retest, if you have already passed, simply to better your time.

A prospective firefighter from Palm Harbor, Florida, has this to say about the physical ability tests:

> All physical ability tests are different, depending on the fire department's equipment and course setup. I've taken physical ability tests for five different municipal fire departments in the last year and a half, and some were much harder than others. Don't be fooled into thinking all physical tests are easy if you happen to take one that doesn't seem very difficult. The next one might be a killer. I'm in great shape, but I just took a test that was a lot harder than the four I'd taken previously. My advice is to do a lot of running to prepare for physical ability tests, because the tough tests really take a lot of endurance.

Many urban fire departments report that the physical ability test is the one step of the process in which the most applicants fail. People come in unprepared; they're simply not strong enough or fast enough to do all the events, while wearing heavy gear, in the time allotted. Female applicants in particular have high failure rates on physical ability tests because some of the events require a lot of upper-body strength.

Be assured that the physical ability test is one area where advance preparation is almost guaranteed to pay off. No matter what your physical condition is, start or continue an exercise program now. You can design your program around the requirements listed in the exam announcement, although any exercise that increases your strength and stamina will help. Because sheer brute force is required to drag a 150-pound dummy or to lift a 50-foot ladder, exercises that increase your strength are particularly important. But you'll also want to include some aerobic exercise such as running or swimming, to improve your stamina and overall fitness as well.

If you're not in great shape, consult a doctor before you begin an exercise program. Start slowly and increase your activity as you go. As you gain strength, start wearing weights on your ankles and wrists, and later add a weighted backpack. To stay motivated, consider working out with a partner; not only is this more fun, but it also helps guard against the temptation to cheat by skipping a day or doing fewer reps.

Physical Ability Exam Tips

- Take advantage of any training sessions or test course walk-throughs the fire department offers; their sole purpose is to help you pass the physical test.
- Start exercising immediately; work on aerobic conditioning and strength training, concentrating on the upper body.
- If you smoke, stop.
- If you're overweight, begin to eat a healthier diet designed to help you lose weight.
- Stay motivated: exercise with a friend, listen to music while working out, give yourself rewards for reaching milestones like shaving a minute off your mile run time or bench-pressing 10 more pounds.

The Background Investigation

Firefighters must be citizens of good character who can get along with both their company and the people they serve. A background investigation is one of the ways a hiring department determines whether an applicant is the kind of person it is looking for. Not all fire departments conduct background investigations, but the ones that do conduct them only on applicants who have passed the written and physical tests.

You may not be alerted that an investigation is taking place, so be sure to answer everything on your application honestly. If your friends, classmates, coworkers, or family give information that contradicts what you've said, you may be dropped from the application process.

Some departments will investigate you in great depth, asking their contacts how long and how well they knew you and what kind of person they found you to be. Did you meet your obligations? How did you deal with problems? Did they find you to be an honest person? Do they know of anything that might affect your fitness to be a firefighter? The references you provided will lead the investigator to other people who knew you, and when the investigator is finished, he or she will have a more complete picture of the kind of person you are. Other fire departments conduct a fairly superficial check, calling your former employers and schools simply to verify the information you provided and to ask some basic questions about your conduct.

A few fire departments include a polygraph, or lie detector test, as part of the background investigation. As long as you've been honest throughout the application process, a lie detector test should not cause you concern. The test is designed to pick up physical changes that occur under stress, as when someone is lying. Nervousness about the test experience is expected, and the test is designed to compensate for the ordinary stress people feel when taking a polygraph test. The test taker asks you a few simple questions before beginning, such as "What is your name?" to establish your baseline response.

The best way to improve your chances of successfully getting through a background investigation is to clean up any previous problems that might give you trouble. You can't change the past, but you can use the present to improve your chances in the future. Pay your old traffic tickets, get that juvenile offense that the lawyer said wouldn't count officially expunged from your record, document your full recovery from a serious illness or your drug-free status since high school. Be prepared to answer honestly about your past mistakes, while showing how you have risen above them and moved on.

The Oral Interview and Selection Board

The selection process in most fire departments includes one or more oral interviews. In some cities, applicants who get this far in the process meet with the fire chief or deputy fire chief, who may conduct something like a regular job interview. One fire department job listing described the interview as including "a discussion of the candidate's education, employment experience, military background, driving history, traffic citations, misdemeanor and/or felony convictions, and other related skills and qualifications." In the interview process, the chief will also be assessing your interpersonal skills, whether you seem honest and relatively comfortable in talking to him or her.

You may face an oral selection board in addition to or in place of your interview with the chief. An oral board is similar to a job interview with a fire chief in that you are asked to answer questions so an assessment can be made about your interpersonal skills, communication skills, judgement and decision-making abilities, respect for diversity, and adaptability. The board consists of two to five people, who may be firefighters, civilian personnel, and/or interview specialists. There is usually some variety in the makeup of the board, which may include officers of various ranks and civilians from the personnel department or from the community.

The way the interview is conducted depends on the practices of the individual department. You may be asked a few standard questions, such as "Why do you want to be a firefighter?" "What qualities do you have that would make you good at this job?" and "Could you describe in detail your physical exercise program?" You may be asked about your background, especially if your application or background investigation raised any questions in the board members' minds. Have answers prepared for any questions you can think of that would be asked about your background, in case they come up during the board interview.

Instead of or in addition to such questions, you may be presented with hypothetical situations to which you will be asked to respond. Situational questions involve circumstances common in fighting fires. A board member may say something like: "After a dwelling fire is under control, you're walking through the building checking its structural soundness. When you walk into the living room, you see a fellow firefighter sticking a gold watch into the pocket of his coat. What would you do?" You would then have to come up with an appropriate response to this situation.

Increasingly, cities have standardized the oral board questions. The same questions are asked of every candidate, and when the interview is over the board rates each candidate on a standard scale. This procedure helps the interviewers reach a somewhat more objective conclusion about the candidates they have interviewed and may result in a score that is included in the factors used to rank candidates in the eligibility list.

A career firefighter from California has this advice to give prospective firefighters who complete an oral interview or an oral board:

> As soon as you leave, take out a pen and paper and write down as many of the questions asked during the session as you can remember. Then, think about your responses to the questions and how you could make them better. Take time to synthesize your responses to those questions and come up with additional ways you can respond in the future. Chances are that you'll be asked similar questions in another interview. This way you can prepare ahead of time for the next interview or oral board that you'll face.

How to Prepare for the Oral Board or Interview

If the fire department you're applying to hands out any material about the oral board, study it carefully. It may tell you what the board is looking for. It may even give you some sample questions you can practice with.

Whether you're facing an oral board or an individual interview, think about your answers to questions you might be asked. You might even try to write your own oral board questions and situations, and write down your answers if you want to. Practice saying them in front of a mirror until you feel comfortable, but don't memorize them. You don't want to sound like you're reciting from a book. Your answers should sound conversational even though you've prepared in advance.

Then enlist friends or family to serve as a mock oral board or interviewer. If you know a practiced public speaker, or someone with interviewing expertise, get him or her to help. Give them your questions, tell them about what you've learned, and then have a practice oral board or interview. Start from the moment you walk into the room. Go through the entire session as if it were the real thing, and then ask your mock board or interviewer for feedback on your performance. It may even help to videotape your mock board session. The camera can reveal things about your body language or habits that you don't even know about.

Oral Board or Interview Tips

- Dress neatly and conservatively, as you would for a business interview.
- Be polite; say *please* and *thank you*, *sir* and *ma'am*.
- Look at board members or interviewers as they speak to you, and listen carefully to what they say.
- Think before you speak; nod or say *okay* to indicate that you understand the question, and then pause for a moment to collect your thoughts before speaking.
- Take a deep breath, relax, and count to five to regain composure if you become nervous.

The Psychological Evaluation

Some cities include a psychological evaluation as part of the firefighter selection process. The fire department wants to make sure that you are emotionally and mentally stable before putting you in a high-stress job in which you have to interact with peers, superiors, and the public. The psychological evaluation is not designed to uncover your deep, dark secrets; its only purpose is to make sure you have the mental and emotional health to do the job.

If your fire department has a psychological evaluation, most likely that means you'll be taking one or two written tests. A few cities have candidates interviewed by a psychologist or a psychiatrist. If you have to take a written psychological test, it is likely to be a standardized multiple-choice or true-false test licensed from a psychological testing company. The Minnesota Multiphasic Personality Inventory (MMPI) is one commonly used test. Such tests typically ask you about your interests, attitudes, and background. They may take one hour or several; the hiring agency will let you know approximately how much time to allot.

If you need to undergo an oral psychological assessment, you'll meet with a psychologist or a psychiatrist, who may be on the hiring agency's staff or an independent contractor. The psychologist may ask you questions about your schooling and jobs, your relationships with family and friends, your habits, and your hobbies. The psychologist may be as interested in the way you answer—whether you come across as open, forthright, and honest—as in the answers themselves.

Don't try to psych out the assessment. The psychologists who designed the written test know more about psyching out tests than you do. They designed the test so that one answer checks against another, to find out whether test takers are lying. Be sure to answer every question openly and honestly, and this part of the process should go smoothly.

The Medical Examination

Before passage of the Americans with Disabilities Act (ADA), many fire departments conducted a medical examination early in the selection process, before the physical ability test. Now, the ADA says it is illegal to do any medical examinations or ask any questions that could reveal an applicant's disability until after a conditional offer of employment has been made. That means that in most jurisdictions you will get such a conditional offer before you are asked to submit to a medical exam.

One exception is the test for use of illegal drugs, which can be administered before a conditional offer of employment. Because firefighters have to be in excellent physical shape and because they are in a position of public trust, the fire department expects you to be drug free. You may have to undergo drug testing periodically throughout your career as a firefighter.

You should know, however, that almost any disability is grounds for disqualification as a firefighter, even under the protections provided by the ADA. Fire fighting requires a high level of physical and mental fitness, and a host of disabilities could prevent a firefighter from fulfilling essential job functions. For instance, a skin condition that requires a man to wear facial hair would disqualify that man from being a firefighter, because facial hair interferes with the proper operation of firefighters' breathing apparatus.

What the Medical Exam Is Like

The medical exam is a thorough physical. The doctor may be on the staff of the hiring agency or someone outside the department with his or her own medical practice. Your blood pressure, temperature, weight, and height will be measured. Your heart and lungs will be listened to and your limbs examined. The doctor will peer into your eyes, ears, nose, and mouth. Your vision and hearing will be tested. Blood and urine will be collected for testing. Because of these tests, you won't know the results of the physical exam right away. You will be notified of the results in writing after the test results come in.

The Waiting Game

You went through the whole process, passed all the tests, did the best you could, and made the eligibility list. The next step is to wait. The Houston Fire Department's application process takes three months, for example, and candidates can wait for a year until their names come up on the eligibility list.

While you are waiting, why not do something to prepare for what you hope is your new career? Do some networking. Talk to firefighters about what the job is really like. Find out if your fire department offers volunteer opportunities or a cadet program. Take a course in first aid or enroll in an EMT program. Even if you don't get called, and even if your rank on the eligibility list doesn't get you a job this time, you'll be better qualified for the next try.

Even though you might be very curious to learn about your standing in the application process, you should resist the temptation to call the fire department for updates about the eligibility list or your chance of getting hired. You might come across as a nuisance to the very people you need to impress; even though you will most likely be talking to a receptionist, you always want to create a good impression with all the people that you come in contact with at the fire department. Many departments have websites or other means of keeping applicants informed about their status. Be sure that you know the correct procedure for obtaining information and follow it. You will demonstrate that you know how to follow protocol, a very important trait for a firefighter.

If at First You Don't Succeed, Part One

The selection process for firefighters is a rigorous one. If you fail one of the steps or do poorly on one of the exams, take time for some serious self-evaluation, so you can do better the next time around. Here are some tips on how you can evaluate your performance on the different steps of the application process.

The Written Test

If you didn't pass the written test, examine the reasons why you didn't do well. Was it just that the format was unfamiliar? Next time, you will know what to expect. Do you need to brush up on some of the skills tested? There are many books designed to help people with basic skills. You might start with the LearningExpress Skill Builder books. (See Appendix C for a list of other helpful texts.) Enlist a teacher or a friend to help you or check out the inexpensive courses offered by local high schools and community colleges. Some fire departments allow you to retest after a waiting period, a period you can use to improve your skills. If the exam isn't being offered again for years, consider trying a different jurisdiction.

The Physical Ability Test

If you don't pass the physical test, your course of action is clear. Increase your daily physical exercise until you know you can do what is required, and then retest or try another jurisdiction.

The Oral Board or Interview

If you don't pass the oral board or interview, try to figure out what the problem was. Do you think your answers were good but perhaps you didn't express them well? Then you need some practice in oral communication. You can take courses or enlist your friends to help you practice.

Did the questions and situations surprise you, so you gave what now seem like inappropriate answers? Then spend time practicing answering similar questions for the next time. Talk to candidates who were successful and ask them what they said. Talk with firefighters you know about what might have been good answers for the questions you were asked. Even if your department doesn't allow you to redo the oral board, you can use what you learn when applying to another fire department.

The Medical Exam

If the medical exam eliminates you, you will usually be notified as to what condition caused the problem. Many conditions are correctable.

Other Reasons

If you don't make the eligibility list and aren't told why, the problem might have been the oral board, the psychological evaluation, or the background investigation. Think of what in your past might lead to questions about your fitness to be a firefighter. Could any of your personal traits or attitudes raise such questions? Is there anything you can do to change these aspects of your past or your personality? If so, you might have a chance when you reapply or apply to another department. If not, you may want to consider another profession.

If you feel you were wrongly excluded on the basis of a psychological evaluation or a background check, most departments have appeals procedures. However, that word *wrongly* is very important. The psychologist or the background investigator almost certainly had to supply a rationale in recommending that the department not hire you. Do you have solid factual evidence that you can use in an administrative hearing to counter such a rationale? If not, you'd be wasting your time and money, as well as the hiring agency's, by making an appeal. Move carefully and get legal advice before you take such a step.

If at First You Don't Succeed, Part Two

If you make the eligibility list, go through the waiting game, and finally aren't selected, don't despair. Think through all the steps of the selection process again and use them to do a critical self-evaluation. Maybe your written, physical, and oral board scores were high enough to pass but not high enough to put you at the top of the list. At the next testing, make sure you're better prepared.

Maybe you had excellent scores that should have put you at the top of the list, and you suspect that you were passed over for someone lower down. That means someone less well qualified was selected while you were not, right? Perhaps. There were probably a lot of people on the list, and a lot of them might have scored high. One more point on a test might have made the difference, or maybe the department had the freedom to pick and choose on the basis of other qualifications. Maybe, in comparison with you, a lot of people on the eligibility list had more education or experience.

There might have been plenty of certified EMTs or paramedics on the list, and they got first crack at the available jobs. It is also possible that members of minority groups and veterans might have been given preference in hiring. Whether or not you think that's fair, you can be assured that it was a conscious decision on the part of the hiring agency; it might even have been mandated from above.

Don't get discouraged. Realize that it may take several tries before you land your dream job. There's a lot of competition out there and not enough openings for everyone to land a job the first time around. Many firefighters have had to persevere for several years before landing a job. A firefighter in Colorado says:

> It took me a lot of time to get on—almost five years, and I had a lot of experience behind me. You need to continually update your education and work on your oral skills. I know people who tried for eight years before they finally made it. It's all worth it in the end. My department just hired a 31-year-old man who has been trying to land a full-time paid position since he was 23, so you can see that it takes time. You have to be patient.

This firefighter's experience is by no means unique. Many firefighters who were recently hired say that it took them a long time to make it into the department they wanted. In fact, a firefighter in California says:

I was recently hired as a firefighter/paramedic with the American Rural Fire Protection District in California. Getting this job was a dream come true. I have been testing for over four years, taking classes, and volunteering my time, but I feel that it has all been worth it. I love my job, and I plan to stay in this department until I retire.

STATE OR FEDERAL WILDLAND FIREFIGHTER SELECTION PROCESS

The selection process for finding new firefighters for state and federal government agencies is usually shorter and less involved than the municipal selection process. Another difference is that the selection process is on a much larger scale, since state and federal agencies normally need to hire a much larger group of firefighters than each local government agency does. Also, most wildland firefighter positions are seasonal, so there tends to be significant turnover in the ranks.

While each state and federal agency has its own selection process, there are some things they have in common. You normally have to pass a physical ability test. For example, a state agency located in Idaho requires candidates to take two physical tests: one test requires applicants to run a mile and a half in 11 minutes; the second test requires applicants to run for three miles with a 45-pound-pack on their back within 45 minutes. Many state and federal agencies also require that a short firefighter training course be completed. These training courses may last anywhere from a few hours to a few days to a week or more.

After being hired, wildland firefighters normally need to pass a one-week training course in fighting wildland fires. Applicants who have not yet been hired can also take the training course, but they need to sign a waiver relieving the training company of responsibility if they have any physical problems during the training course. Most week-long training courses offer students what is commonly referred to as a *pink card* or *red card*, a small card that wildland firefighters carry with them that specifies their firefighting qualifications.

IN THE NEWS

Wildfires are occurring more often and becoming more intense, according to some U.S. government experts. Scientists say that the worst drought in 500 years and a warming climate have led the average number of major forest fires in western states to become four times more prevalent between 1970 and 2006. In 2005, possibly the worst fire season in history, more than 8.53 million acres across the country burned.

How to Apply

For jobs with state agencies, begin your search on the Internet, with the listing for the department of natural resources or the forest service in the state(s) you are interested in working in. There are also employment opportunities listed on www.geocities.com/Yosemite/Gorge/5561/state.html. Associations such as the National Association of State Fire Marshals (NASFM) and the National Association of State Foresters may also be good sources of information.

Most federal jobs are offered through the Office of Personnel Management (OPM). You can visit its website (http://jobsearch.usajobs.opm.gov/series_search.aps) and search for firefighting jobs by typing in the Standard Occupational Series Code #0462. A recent search at this site listed openings with the U.S. Forest Service (Department of Agriculture); Bureau of Indian Affairs, National Park Service, Bureau of Land Management, and Fish and Wildlife Service (all Department of the Interior); and the Field Operating Office of the Secretary of the Army and the Air Force Personnel Center (both Department of Defense). For all federal positions, you may apply using the Application for Federal Employment, the Optional Application for Federal Employment (OF-612), or a resume that includes all the information requested by the publication entitled *Applying for a Federal Job* (OF-512). Application procedures are detailed on the OPM's website. Appendix B lists all the federal agencies that hire firefighters, with contact information.

The U.S. Forest Service (USFS) operates regional offices throughout the country that may be contacted for job opportunities. Check the list below for the office(s) near where you'd like to work, and call or write for more information.

USFS NORTHERN REGION (R-1)

Federal Building

PO Box 7669

Missoula, MT 59807

406-329-3510

USFS ROCKY MOUNTAIN REGION (R-2)

740 Simms Street

Golden, CO 80401

303-275-5350

USFS SOUTHWESTERN REGION (R-3)

333 Broadway SE

Albuquerque, NM 87102

505-842-3292

USFS INTERMOUNTAIN REGION (R-4)

Federal Building

324 25th Street

Ogden, UT 84401

801-625-5306

USFS PACIFIC SOUTHWEST REGION (R-5)

1323 Club Drive

Vallejo, CA 94592

707-562-8737

USFS PACIFIC NORTHWEST REGION (R-6)

333 SW First Avenue

PO Box 3623

Portland, OR 97208

503-808-2468

USFS SOUTHERN REGION (R-8)

Southern Area Coordination Center

1200 Ashwood Parkway Ste 230

Atlanta, GA 30338

679-320-3000

USFS EASTERN REGION (R-9)

626 E Wisconsin Avenue

Milwaukee, WI 53202

414-297-3600

USFS ALASKA REGION (R-10)

PO Box 21628

Juneau, AK 99802

907-586-8806

USFS NORTHEASTERN AREA—STATE AND PRIVATE FORESTRY

Office of the Director

11 Campus Boulevard Suite 200

Newtown Square, PA 19073

610-557-4103

For seasonal temporary positions, the best times to inquire are during the months of December and January. Contact a Bureau of Land Management, Forest Service, or National Park Service Human Resources Office closest to the location in which you want to work; or look for openings listed on the OPM Website.

Sample Application

See the sample application on pages 70–71 to get an idea of what you might be filling out as an initial step in becoming a federal firefighter. This application is provided as a sample only and cannot be used to submit for a job. You need to get an original application form from the appropriate department when you're ready to apply. However, you can read through the sample to find out what sort of information you'll be asked to provide and to practice filling out the application. Don't underestimate this step. Filling out the application neatly and accurately can make or break your quest for employment, because it's a key part of the employment process.

MILITARY FIREFIGHTER SELECTION PROCESS

If you would like to go the military route to becoming a firefighter, you need to join the military as the first step of the selection process. You'll need to meet the basic requirements for entering the military (see Chapter 1 for a list of minimum requirements). The next step is to talk to military recruiters to find out how you can get a guarantee of being trained and placed in the fire protection field within the military. You must meet a number of specific requirements in order to qualify for a guaranteed firefighter career area; check with your local recruiting agent to find out exactly what steps you need to take.

The Armed Services Vocational Aptitude Battery (ASVAB)

Many high schools and postsecondary schools offer the ASVAB test to students. It is also offered at various locations nationwide by the military itself.

Ask your local recruiter when and where you can take this test. But before you take the test, be sure to prepare for it. You need to achieve a score of 39 or higher on this test in order to be eligible for a firefighting career. There are several test-preparation books that lead you through the test step by step and give you plenty of practice taking sample tests. See Appendix C for helpful test-preparation books that you can use to increase your score on the all-important ASVAB test.

The Enlistment Agreement

If you achieve a high enough score on the ASVAB test and pass all other requirements, the branch of the military you want to work in may guarantee in writing that your career area will be within the fire protection field as a part of your enlistment agreement. Be sure you read the entire enlistment agreement very carefully and ask any questions that you have before you sign it. It is a legally binding document, so don't sign it without serious thought.

You'll also need to decide the length of your enlistment before you sign on the dotted line. If you plan to leave the military to join a municipal fire department as soon as possible, then you'll want to enlist for the shortest possible time while gaining the most experience you can.

Military Training

After you enlist in the military, you'll undergo basic training for several weeks. If you have fire protection guaranteed as your career area, you'll then be given additional training as a firefighter before being assigned to a military fire department or base.

The Navy offers certified apprenticeship programs for some specialties within the firefighting occupation. The Air Force offers a 13-week fire protection training program at the Goodfellow Air Force Base in San Angelo, Texas, for military members who will be serving as firefighters in the Marines, the Army, or the Air Force. You may be able to achieve college credit for some of your training courses from the Community College of the Air Force.

You may apply for most Federal jobs with a résumé, an Optional Application for Federal Employment (OF 612), or other written format. If your résumé or application does not provide all the information requested on this form and in the job vacancy announcement, you may lose consideration for a job. Type or print clearly in black ink. Help speed the selection process by keeping your application brief and sending only the requested information. If essential to attach additional pages, include your name and job announcement number on each page.

- Information on Federal employment and the latest information about educational and training provisions are available at www.usajobs.gov or via interactive voice response system: (703) 724-1850 or TDD (978) 461-8404.

- Upon request from the employing Federal agency, you must provide documentation or proof that your degree(s) is from a school accredited by an accrediting body recognized by the Secretary, U.S. Department of Education, or that your education meets the other provisions outlined in the OPM Operating Manual. It will be your responsibility to secure the documentation that verifies that you attended and earned your degree(s) from this accredited institution(s) (e.g., official transcript). Federal agencies will verify your documentation.

  For a list of postsecondary educational institutions and programs accredited by accrediting agencies and state approval agencies recognized by the U.S. Secretary of Education, refer to the U.S. Department of Education Office of Postsecondary Education website at http://www.ope.ed.gov/accreditation/.

  For information on Educational and Training Provisions or Requirements, refer to the OPM Operating Manual available at http://www.opm.gov/qualifications/SEC-II/s2-e4.asp.

- If you served on active duty in the United States Military and were discharged or released from active duty in the armed forces under honorable conditions, you may be eligible for veterans' preference. To receive preference, if your service began after October 15, 1976, you must have a Campaign Badge, Expeditionary Medal, or a service-connected disability. Veterans' preference is not a factor for Senior Executive Service jobs or when competition is limited to status candidates (current or former career or career-conditional Federal employees).

- Most Federal jobs require United States citizenship and also that males over age 18 born after December 31, 1959, have registered with the Selective Service System or have an exemption.

- The law generally prohibits public officials from appointing, promoting, or recommending their relatives.

- Federal annuitants (military and civilian) may have their salaries or annuities reduced. Every employee must pay any valid delinquent debt or the agency may garnish their salary.

- Send your application to the office announcing the vacancy. If you have questions, contact the office identified in the announcement.

How to Apply

1. **Review** the listing of current vacancies.
2. **Decide** which jobs, pay range, and locations interest you.
3. **Follow instructions** provided in the vacancy announcement including any additional forms that are required.
   - You may apply for most jobs with a resume, this form, or any other written format; **all applications must include the information requested in the vacancy announcement as well as information required for all applications for Federal employment** (see below):
   - The USAJOBS website features an online résumé builder. This is a free service that allows you to create a résumé, submit it electronically (for some vacancy announcements), and save it online for use in the future.

Certain information is required to evaluate your qualifications and determine if you meet legal requirements for Federal employment. If your resume or application does not include all the required information as specified below, the agency may not consider you for the vacancy. Help speed the selection process - submit a concise resume' or application and send only the required material.

Information required for all applications for Federal employment:

Job Vacancy Specifics

- Announcement number, title and grade(s) of the job you are applying for

Personal Information

- Full name, mailing address (with zip code) and day and evening phone numbers (with area code) and email address, if applicable
- Social Security Number
- *Country of citizenship (most Federal jobs require U.S. citizenship)*
- Veterans' preference
- Reinstatement eligibility (for former Federal employees)
- Highest Federal civilian grade held (including job series and dates held)
- Selective Service (if applicable)

Work Experience

- Provide the following information for your paid and volunteer work experience related to the job you are applying for:
  - ▶ job title (include job series and grade if Federal)
  - ▶ duties and accomplishments
  - ▶ employer's name and address
  - ▶ supervisor's name and telephone number - indicate if supervisor may be contacted
  - ▶ starting and ending dates (month and year)
  - ▶ hours per week
  - ▶ salary

U.S. Office of Personnel Management
Previous edition usable

NSN 7540-01-351-9178
50612-101

Page 1 of 4

OF 612
Revised June 2006

68

Education

- High School
  - ▶ Name, city, and State (Zip code if known)
  - ▶ Date of diploma or GED
- Colleges or universities
  - ▶ Name, city, and State (Zip code if known)
  - ▶ Majors
  - ▶ Type and year of degrees received. (If no degree, show total credits earned and indicate whether semester or quarter hours.)
- Do not attach a copy of your transcript unless requested
- Do not list degrees received based solely on life experience or obtained from schools with little or no academic standards

Upon request from the employing Federal agency, you must provide documentation or proof that your degree(s) is from a school accredited by an accrediting body recognized by the Secretary, U.S. Department of Education, or that your education meets the other provisions outlined in the OPM Operating Manual. It will be your responsibility to secure the documentation that verifies that you attended and earned your degree(s) from this accredited institution(s) (e.g., official transcript). Federal agencies will verify your documentation.

For a list of postsecondary educational institutions and programs accredited by accrediting agencies and state approval agencies recognized by the U.S. Secretary of Education, refer to the U.S. Department of Education Office of Postsecondary Education website at http://www.ope.ed.gov/accreditation/.

For information on Educational and Training Provisions or Requirements, refer to the OPM Operating Manual available at http://www.opm.gov/qualifications/SEC-II/s2-e4.asp.

Other Education Completed

- School name, city, and State (Zip code if known)
  - ▶ Credits earned and Majors
  - ▶ Type and year of degrees received. (If no degree, show total credits earned and indicate whether semester or quarter hours.)
- Do not list degrees received based solely on life experience or obtained from schools with little or no academic standards

Other Qualifications

- Job-related:
  - ▶ Training (title of course and year)
  - ▶ Skills (e.g., other languages, computer software/hardware, tools, machinery, typing speed, etc.)
  - ▶ Certificates or licenses (current only). Include type of license or certificate, date of latest license, and State or other licensing agency
  - ▶ Honors, awards, and special accomplishments, (e.g., publications, memberships in professional honor societies, leadership activities, public speaking and performance awards) (Give dates but do not send documents unless requested)

Any Other Information Specified in the Vacancy Announcement

Privacy Act Statement

The U.S. Office of Personnel Management and other Federal agencies rate applicants for Federal jobs under the authority of sections 1104, 1302, 3301, 3304, 3320, 3361, 3393, and 3394 of title 5 of the United States Code. We need the information requested in this form and in the associated vacancy announcements to evaluate your qualifications. Other laws require us to ask about citizenship, military service, etc. In order to keep your records in order, we request your Social Security Number (SSN) under the authority of Executive Order 9397 which requires the SSN for the purpose of uniform, orderly administration of personnel records. Failure to furnish the requested information may delay or prevent action on your application. We use your SSN to seek information about you from employers, schools, banks, and others who know you. We may use your SSN in studies and computer matching with other Government files. If you do not give us your SSN or any other information requested, we cannot process your application. Also, incomplete addresses and ZIP Codes will slow processing. We may confirm information from your records with prospective nonfederal employers concerning tenure of employment, civil service status, length of service, and date and nature of action for separation as shown on personnel action forms of specifically identified individuals.

Public Burden Statement

We estimate the public reporting burden for this collection will vary from 20 to 240 minutes with an average of 90 minutes per response, including time for reviewing instructions, searching existing data sources, gathering data, and completing and reviewing the information. Send comments regarding the burden statement or any other aspect of the collection of information, including suggestions for reducing this burden to the U.S. Office of Personnel Management (OPM), OPM Forms Officer, Washington, DC 20415-7900. The OMB number, 3206-0219, is currently valid. OPM may not collect this information and you are not required to respond, unless this number is displayed. Do not send completed application forms to this address; follow directions provided in the vacancy announcement(s).

THE FEDERAL GOVERNMENT IS AN EQUAL OPPORTUNITY EMPLOYER

U.S. Office of Personnel Management
Previous edition usable

NSN 7540-01-351-9178
50612-101

OF 61:
Revised June 2006

Page 2 of 4

69

OPTIONAL APPLICATION FOR FEDERAL EMPLOYMENT - OF 612

Form Approved
OMB No. 3206-0219

Section A - Applicant Information

Use Standard State Postal Codes (abbreviations). If outside the United States of America, and you do not have a military address, type or print "OV" in the State field (Block 6c) and fill in the Country field (Block 6e) below, leaving the Zip Code field (Block 6d) blank.

1. Job title in announcement	2. Grade(s) applying for	3. Announcement number

4a. Last name	4b. First and middle names	5. Social Security Number

6a. Mailing address	7. Phone numbers (include area code if within the United States of America) 7a. Daytime

6b. City	6c. State	6d. Zip Code	7b. Evening

6e. Country (if not within the United States of America)

8. Email address (if available)

Section B - Work Experience

Describe your paid and non-paid work experience related to the job for which you are applying. Do not attach job description.

1. Job title (if Federal, include series and grade)

2. From (mm/yyyy)	3. To (mm/yyyy)	4. Salary per $	5. Hours per week

6. Employer's name and address	7. Supervisor's name and phone number 7a. Name
	7b. Phone

8. May we contact your current supervisor?   Yes ☐   No ☐
If we need to contact your current supervisor before making an offer, we will contact you first.

9. Describe your duties, accomplishments and related skills (if you need to attach additional pages, include your name, address, and job announcement number)

Section C - Additional Work Experience

1. Job title (if Federal, include series and grade)

2. From (mm/yyyy)	3. To (mm/yyyy)	4. Salary per $	5. Hours per week

6. Employer's name and address	7. Supervisor's name and phone number 7a. Name
	7b. Phone

8. May we contact your current supervisor?   Yes ☐   No ☐
If we need to contact your current supervisor before making an offer, we will contact you first.

9. Describe your duties, accomplishments and related skills (if you need to attach additional pages, include your name, address, and job announcement number)

U.S. Office of Personnel Management
Previous edition usable

NSN 7540-01-351-9178
50612-10
Page 3 of 4

OF 612
Revised June 2006

Section D - Education

Upon request from the employing Federal agency, you must provide documentation or proof that your degree(s) is from a school accredited by an accrediting body recognized by the Secretary, U. S. Department of Education, or that your education meets the other provisions outlined in the OPM Operating Manual. It will be your responsibility to secure the documentation that verifies that you attended and earned your degree(s) from this accredited institution(s) (e.g., official transcript). Federal agencies will verify your documentation.

For a list of postsecondary educational institutions and programs accredited by accrediting agencies and state approval agencies recognized by the U.S. Secretary of Education, refer to the U.S. Department of Education Office of Postsecondary Education website at http://www.ope.ed.gov/accreditation/.

For information on Educational and Training Provisions or Requirements, refer to the OPM Operating Manual available at http://www.opm.gov/qualifications/SEC-II/s2-e4.asp.

Do not list degrees received based solely on life experience or obtained from schools with little or no academic standards.

1. Last High School (HS)/GED school. Give the school's name, city, state, ZIP Code (if known), and year diploma or GED received:

2. Mark highest level completed: Some HS ☐   HS/GED ☐   Associate ☐   Bachelor ☐   Master ☐   Doctoral ☐

3. Colleges and universities attended. Do not attach a copy of your transcript unless requested.			Total Credits Earned		Major(s)	Degree (if any), Year Received
			Semester	Quarter		
3a. Name						
City	State	Zip Code				
3b. Name						
City	State	Zip Code				
3c. Name						
City	State	Zip Code				

Section E - Other Education Completed

Do not list degrees received based solely on life experience or obtained from schools with little or no academic standards.

Section F - Other Qualifications

License or Certificate	Date of Latest License or Certificate	State or Other Licensing Agency
1f.		
2f.		

Section G - Other Qualifications

Job-related training courses (give title and year). Job-related skills (other languages, computer software/hardware, tools, machinery, typing speed, etc.). Job-related honors, awards, and special accomplishments (publications, memberships in professional/honor societies, leadership activities, public speaking, and performance awards). Give dates, but do not send documents unless requested.

Section H - General

1a. Are you a U.S. citizen?   Yes ☐   No ☐   →   1b. If no, give the Country of your citizenship

2a. Do you claim veterans' preference?   Yes ☐   No ☐   →   If yes, mark your claim of 5 or 10 points below.

2b. 5 points   ☐ →   Attach your Report of Separation from Active Duty (DD 214) or other proof.

2c. 10 points   ☐ →   Attach an Application for 10-Point Veterans' Preference (SF 15) and proof required.

3. Check this box if you are an adult male born on or after January 1st 1960, and you registered for Selective Service between the ages of 18 through 25 → ☐

4. Were you ever a Federal civilian employee?   Yes ☐   No ☐   →   If yes, list highest civilian grade for the following:

4a. Series	4b. Grade	4c. From (mm/yyyy)	4d. To (mm/yyyy)

5a. Are you eligible for reinstatement based on career or career-conditional Federal status?   Yes ☐   No ☐
If requested in the vacancy announcement, attach Notification of Personnel Action (SF 50), as proof.

5b. Are you eligible under the ICTAP*?   Yes ☐   No ☐
*ICTAP (Interagency Career Transition Assistance Plan): A participant in this plan is a current or former federal employee displaced from a Federal agency. To be eligible, you must have received a formal notice of separation such as a RIF separation notice. If you are an ICTAP eligible, normally you will be provided priority consideration for vacancies within your commuting area for which you apply and are well qualified.

Section I - Applicant Certification

I certify that, to the best of my knowledge and belief, all of the information on and attached to this application is true, correct, complete, and made in good faith. I understand that false or fraudulent information on or attached to this application may be grounds for not hiring me or for firing me after I begin work, and may be punishable by fine or imprisonment. I understand that any information I give may be investigated.

1a. Signature	1b. Date (mm/dd/yyyy)

Previous edition usable
U.S. Office of Personnel Management

NSN 7540-01-351-9178
50612-10
Page 4 of 4

OF 612
Revised June 2006

71

PRIVATE COMPANY FIREFIGHTER SELECTION PROCESS

Private fire companies are the newest employers within the fire protection field. There are two types of private fire companies: large corporations that employ their own firefighters to protect their equipment on-site and companies that offer fire protection service to a number of clients or in a specific geographic area. Private fire companies offer their services only when and where they are contracted by others to do so.

Companies with On-Site Firefighters

There are hundreds of large companies that hire firefighters or other fire protection specialists to work on-site to protect the company's equipment and other assets. Due to the size and high cost of the equipment at these companies, it's worth the expense of hiring an on-site crew to manage their fire prevention and suppression program. Some examples of companies that hire on-site firefighters or who contract with private fire companies to obtain on-site firefighters are Port Columbus International Airport in Columbus, Ohio; the Federal Express National Operations Center in Memphis, Tennessee; the Hughes Missile System in Arizona; and Boeing, which has several locations and subsidiaries nationwide.

Here is a sample job description from a private company looking for a fire protection specialist:

Fire Protection Engineer

Job Code 23630

The fundamental reason this classification exists is to review building plans and inspect existing structures to ensure conformance to fire protection codes and standards and to assist in writing and updating fire protection codes. Incumbents analyze industrial, commercial, and public buildings and other structures before and after construction; evaluate the fire resistance of structures, taking into consideration the usage and contents of building; evaluate the availability of water supplies and water delivery; and evaluate entrance/exit capabilities. Responsibilities include making recommendations for changes in design, materials, or equipment, such as structural components protection, fire protection equipment, alarm systems, and fire-extinguishing devices and systems. Work involves considerable coordination with the Fire Department, Development Services Department, and other departments regarding the development and enforcement of fire protection codes. Some positions may be assigned supervisory responsibility over clerical and professional employees. Work is accomplished with considerable independence within broad policy outlines and is reviewed through evaluation of reports and conferences by a Deputy Fire Chief, Assistant Fire Chief, or Fire Chief.

Essential Functions

- provide technical assistance to architects, contractors, and other private industry personnel in interpreting and complying with fire codes and standards
- recommend changes in fire codes
- review construction site plans and building plans for compliance with fire protection codes and standards
- evaluate the fire resistance of buildings and structures
- determine whether water availability and water delivery systems are adequate to protect buildings
- demonstrate continuous effort to improve operations, decrease turnaround times, streamline work processes, and work cooperatively and jointly to provide quality seamless customer service

Required Knowledge, Skills, and Abilities

Knowledge of

- building construction, design, and materials as related to fire prevention and fire control
- fire codes and regulations
- fire detection, fire alarm, and fire suppression systems

Ability to

- perform a broad range of supervisory responsibilities
- produce written documents with clearly organized thought using proper English sentence construction, punctuation, and grammar
- communicate orally with customers, clients, and the public in face-to-face, one-on-one settings, in group settings, and using a telephone
- observe or monitor objects to determine compliance with prescribed operating or safety standards
- keep current on city fire codes and ordinances

- comprehend and make inferences from written materials such as fire codes and ordinances
- use graphic instructions such as blueprints, layouts, or other visual aids
- move light objects (under 20 pounds) short distances (20 feet or less)
- enter data or information into a terminal, PC, or other keyboard device
- work cooperatively with other city employees and the public
- work safely without presenting a direct threat to self or others.

Additional Requirements

- Some positions will require the performance of other essential and marginal functions, depending upon work location, assignment, or shift.
- Some positions require the use of personal or city vehicles on city business. Individuals must be physically capable of operating the vehicles safely, possess a valid driver's license, and have an acceptable driving record. Use of a personal vehicle for city business will be prohibited if the employee is not authorized by the city-designated physician to drive a city vehicle or if the employee does not have personal insurance coverage.
- One year of experience in fire protection engineering and a bachelor's degree in fire protection engineering or a related field is required. Other combinations of experience and education that meet the minimum requirements may be substituted for this requirement.

Companies Offering Fire Protection/Suppression Services

A growing number of companies offer fire protection and/or suppression services to private and commercial sites, communities, wildlands, and airports. One example is Rural/Metro Corporation, which currently provides fire protection services to approximately 400 communities and responds to more than 1 million calls annually. To join its reserve program, from which firefighters are selected, applicants must

▶ be at least 21 years old
▶ possess a high school diploma or GED
▶ pass a physical agility test

▶ have an acceptable driving record

▶ pass a drug-screening test

▶ pass a written exam

Once applicants join the reserve program, they need to attend a fire academy on weekends and they can begin going on fire calls after completing a certain amount of training. While firefighters are members of the reserve program, they receive minimum wage for the fire calls they go on. Graduates from the academy are granted a Firefighter II certificate. For reserve firefighters who get hired as full-time career firefighters with Rural/Metro in Louisiana, the starting annual salary is approximately $35,000. Contact Rural/Metro by e-mail at justin_parker@metro.com or call 1-800-352-2309.

Wackenhut is another company that employs hundreds of full-time fire and EMS personnel. It provides fire protection, fire prevention, and emergency response services to commercial facilities such as the Kennedy Space Center, industrial facilities such as Saturn Corporation and Nissan Manufacturing Corporation, airports, and municipal locations that include towns, cities, and counties. Contact Wackenhut at its website: www.wackenhutservices.com.

Alpine Wildfire Services, whose main offices are in Reno, Nevada, provides emergency wildland fire suppression services as well as extended mop-up. Most of its staff are former federal firefighters, but it also trains employees through classes that meet the minimum National Wildfire Coordinating Group (NWCG) guidelines and regulations. Alpine Wildfire Services can be contacted at 39835 McCarrran Boulevard #437, Reno, Nevada 89502.

Other companies that hire out firefighter services are those that provide aerial firefighting. The following is a list of many of these employers, along with contact information.

Multiengine Air Tanker Companies

AERO-FLITE, INC.

Matt Ziomek

4700 Flight Line Drive

Kingman, AZ 86401

520-757-1002

Fax: 520-757-2951

E-mail: aerodc4@ctza.com

AERO UNION CORPORATION

Terry Unsworth

100 Lockheed Avenue

Chico, CA 95973-9098

530-896-3000

Fax: 350-893-8585

ALAMOGORDO-WHITE SANDS REGIONAL AIRPORT

Airport Coordinator

3500 Airport Rd.

Alamogordo, NM 88311

575-439-4110

ARDCO, INC.

Gary Garrett

HC Box 277

Tucson, AZ 85735

520-883-4119

Fax: 520-883-5858

E-mail: ARDCOINC@aol.com

BUTLER AIRCRAFT COMPANY

Cal Butler

1050 SE Sisters Avenue

Redmond, OR 97756-8615

541-548-8166

Fax: 541-548-0863

E-mail: ButlerAcft@aol.com

HIRTH AIR TANKERS

Connie Hirth

160 Airport Road

Johnson County Airport

Buffalo, WY 82834-9357

307-684-7160

Fax: 307-684-7160

INTERNATIONAL AIR RESPONSE

PO Box 67

6100 North Coolidge Airport Road

Coolidge, AZ 85228

520-723-6555

Fax: 520-723-6550

E-mail: info@internationalairresponse.com

www.internationalairresponse.com

NEPTUNE AVIATION SERVICES, INC.

Kristen Schloemer

2 Corporate Way

Missoula, MT 59808

Fax: 406-542-3222

T.B.M., INC.

PO Box 868

Tulare, CA 93275

559-686-3476

Fax: 559-686-3477

Helitanker Companies

ERICKSON AIR-CRANE COMPANY

PO Box 3247

3100 Willow Springs Road

Central Point, OR 97502

541-664-7615

800-424-2413

Fax: 541-664-7613

HEAVY LIFT HELICOPTERS, INC.

19322 Central Road

Apple Valley, CA 92307

760-240-1074

Fax: 760-240-1202

Single-Engine Air Tanker Companies

DOWNSTOWN AERO

Curt Nixholm

339 Harding Highway

Vineland, NJ 08360-9154

856-697-3300

Fax: 856-697-2132

E-mail: FireCats1@aol.com

QUEEN BEE AIR SPECIALTIES, INC.

Chuck Kemper

PO Box 245

136 N Yellowstone Highway

Rigby, ID 83442-0245

208-745-7654 or

800-736-6754

Sustaining Members

AIR TRACTOR, INC.

PO Box 485

Olney, TX 76374-0485

940-564-5616

Fax: 940-564-5612

email: airmail@airtractor.com

ARNOLD KOLB

PO Box 1828

Alamogordo, NM 88310-1828

505-439-5621

Fax: 505-437-8194

BIGHORN AIRWAYS, INC.

PO Box 4037

912 West Brundage Lane

Sheridan, WY 82801

307-672-3421

Fax: 307-672-8580

PRECISION ENGINES

CORPORATION

Dave Cort

3220 100th Street SW

Everett, WA 98204

425-347-2800

Fax: 425-353-9431

How to Apply

The biggest challenge in applying for jobs with private fire companies is to find out about job openings and the names of companies that are looking for firefighters. After you've tried contacting one or more of the companies listed in the preceding section, try word of mouth. Ask any of the firefighters or fire instructors you know if they can give you possible leads on private fire company names and locations. You might want to consider subscribing to a firefighter recruitment service that includes private fire companies in its listings (see Appendix A for contact information).

Another way to find out about these jobs is to scour your local newspapers and phone books and ask your local public librarian for information about companies that appear to have a need for fire services, such as oil refineries or shipyards or companies in the chemical, aircraft, and aerospace industries. Once you locate such companies, call their human resources department and inquire about possible openings.

JOB OPPORTUNITIES FOR THOSE LEAVING THE MILITARY

There are both direct and indirect benefits for people leaving the military who are seeking firefighting positions. An indirect benefit is that firefighter training and experience in the military is highly valued. Prospective employers may look more favorably on the applications of people who have been in the military, because of the high quality of firefighting training and experience those applicants received while serving in the military. The military's focus on the importance of teamwork and following orders is highly esteemed by many municipal fire chiefs. Members of the military who learn teamwork skills and who learn to follow a commander's orders while in the line of duty are considered well equipped to do the same in a fire department; therefore, if you have a military background, it is a plus for you.

A more direct benefit occurs for select groups of people—and, in some cases, their spouses—who leave the military. This direct benefit is normally referred to as veterans' preference. The preference may give job applicants extra points, ranging from 5 to 15, on a portion of the testing process. For example, if you meet the eligibility requirements, you could score a 100 on the written exam and be given an additional 5 points for your active military duty, which would result in a score of 105. Such a high score would most likely put you at or near the top of the eligibility list for most fire departments. Many military members who served in Operation Desert Storm are eligible for this direct benefit. Specific information about who qualifies for veterans' preference should be clearly spelled out in your job application. For more information on veterans' preference programs, you can call 912-757-3000 and select *Federal Employment Topics* and then *Veterans*.

USING THE INTERNET TO HELP LAND THE JOB YOU WANT

The Internet has become a valuable resource for locating information about firefighting and for landing a job in this coveted field. We have already listed many websites for employers, ranging from small, private companies to the federal government. Aside from connecting with potential employers directly, there are other job search services you should be aware of.

Sites of interest to job seekers in the fire protection field include those of fire-related professional associations, bookstores, specific fire departments, recruitment agencies, and many others. The following section enumerates key fire-related websites that can help maximize your chances of landing the perfect job, from giving you general information on the different careers available, to offering books for sale and bulletin boards to post questions, to giving you inside news from experienced firefighters across the country. You will find that many of these sites contain links to other sites that may also be of interest.

Professional Associations

Professional associations can give you general information about the fire service industry as well as specific information on a variety of topics within the field of fire protection. Check out the following websites for a variety of information, ranging from newsletters and fire statistics to educational resources and fire news.

www.nfpa.org

> This site contains the latest information about the National Fire Protection Association (NFPA), its departments, publications, seminars, and educational programs. The NFPA, which was organized in 1896, is the largest private organization devoted to fire protection. This site also has a good selection of links to other fire-related websites.

www.iaff.org

> This is the website for the International Association of Fire Fighters (IAFF). It offers legislative news, political actions, regulatory updates, a calendar of events, and other information of interest to firefighters.

www.usfa.fema.gov

> The U.S. Fire Administration (USFA) website offers a wealth of information about firefighting. The USFA was established by Congress in 1974; its mission is to provide leadership, coordination, and support for the nation's fire prevention and control, fire training and education, and emergency medical services activities. This website offers extensive free publications on a range of firefighting topics.

See Appendix B for more listings of professional associations and other organizations of interest to firefighters.

Employment Recruitment Companies

These websites offer employment recruiting information for a fee to prospective firefighters and to firefighters looking for promotional opportunities. Review each company carefully before you commit to subscribing to a recruitment service. Each offers slightly different services and they all charge different fees. Recruitment companies can be especially helpful to prospective firefighters who are looking for openings in parts of the country other than where they live. Some of these sites also contain free fire-related information at their websites, such as bulletin boards, bookstores, links to other sites, and chat rooms.

www.firecareers.com

The Perfect Firefighter Candidate is a recruitment company that offers information about job openings, filing deadlines, salary, requirements, and whom to contact or how to get involved in the testing process for each job listed. You can subscribe to a monthly e-mail notification service to get job information on all levels of jobs, from firefighter to fire chief. The website also offers a bulletin board, chat room, and books and other products for sale. New additions are scheduled to be added to this site.

www.publicsafetyrecruitment.com

Public Safety Recruitment was established in 1993. It provides information from thousands of paid fire departments and EMS agencies across the nation. The monthly newsletter, weekly e-mail service, and 800 telephone numbers offer prospective applicants the names of recruiting agencies and detailed information about potential jobs, including contact information. Check its website for its latest fee schedule. It also offers an online bookstore where you can view descriptions of and order helpful firefighting books. You can e-mail your questions or comments to info@publicsafetyrecruitment.com.

www.ifpra.com

This website of the International Fire and Police Recruitment Administration (IFPRA), offers recruiting information to firefighter applicants.

See Appendix A for a more extensive list of fire service-specific employment resources.

Books, Videos, and Other Products

Here are some websites that offer fire-related books, videos, audio recordings, and other products of interest to firefighters and prospective firefighters.

www.firebooks.com
> This site contains a firefighter's online bookstore. You can order a free catalog to see what books it offers or order directly from the site.

www.ifsta.org/catalog/prevention.html
> A website for the International Fire Service Training Association (IFSTA) that offers a list of the 77 manuals it publishes.

www.fire-police-ems.com
> This is the website for FSP Books and Videos, a company that sells books, videos, and other materials related to fire, police, and EMS. You can order directly from this site.

Wildland Firefighter Information

The following sites offer information useful for prospective or active wildfire firefighters on the state or federal level.

www.nifc.gov
> The National Interagency Fire Center (NIFC), in Boise, Idaho, includes the nation's primary logistical support center for wildland fire suppression. Working with state and local agencies, NIFC provides national response to wildfires and other emergencies and serves as a focal point for wildland fire information and technology.

www.blm.gov
> This Bureau of Land Management website discusses how to obtain federal firefighting jobs and offers a list of state agencies, including contact information.

www.wildfiremag.com
> This is the website of *Wildfire* magazine, which is published by the International Association of Wildland Fire. This magazine discusses wildland

fire safety and current issues in wildland fire and is written by firefighters, fire managers, and experts in aviation and crew resource management.

Other Fire-Related Websites

Here are a variety of websites that contain information related to firefighting. You can look for job leads, keep up with industry changes, look for networking contacts, and stay abreast of fire-related news by accessing these sites on a regular basis.

www.rescue1.com/fire411.htm
> Rescue One offers a website containing information related to EMS, police, and fire occupations. It links you directly to the fire headquarters page, which contains a list of more than 30 links to other fire-related websites, including specific fire departments across the nation, recruitment companies, federal and state government agencies, professional associations, and fire reports.

www.firefighting.com
> This is an interactive website that offers news, press releases, and products. Current firefighters are invited to post information and news on the site.

www.september11.archive.org
> This site includes the Library of Congress archive and analysis.

Appendix C contains dozens of additional resources related to firefighting careers.

Job Links

www.fs.fed.us/fire
> The U.S. Forest Service website is excellent and contains job links, fire news, maps, descriptions of firefighter jobs, and qualifications for jobs.

www.wildfiretrainingnet.com/links/cat27.shtml
> Free wildfire job links, bookstore, vendors, and library make this website a great resource for wildland firefighters.

www1.firejobs.com

The National Directory of Emergency Services website contains job listings, career tips, and links to fire service-related sites of interest.

INSIDE TRACK

Thomas J. Kichemaster II
Volunteer: Lieutenant/EMT/Fire Investigator
Philomath Rural Fire Protection District #4
Philomath, Oregon

I have been a volunteer firefighter/EMT for 16 years, 11 with the Philomath RFPD. I actually fell into it by accident. When I was 17 years old, I happened to be the first person to find a small grass fire that was quickly growing, and I decided to do something about it. I had someone call 911 and then I got a shovel and started to "line" the fire. The fire department showed up, I talked to them for a few minutes and found out they were a volunteer department and were looking for some people, and the rest is history.

I like to help people, and that is the best part of being a firefighter. I love to educate the public on ways to make themselves and loved ones safer, and I spend most of my time on these fire prevention activities. Public education has taught people just how dangerous fire is, and since I have been a volunteer I have seen less and less fires. The worst part of being a firefighter is the death and destruction I see.

As an investigator, my main duty is determining how and why a fire started—this includes interviewing witnesses, examining the fire scene, and managing scene safety and reports. I also have responsibility for the crews under my command on a call, and I'm the president of the district's volunteers.

Being a volunteer, I am on call 24 hours a day, seven days a week—I carry my pager with me all the time. Of course if I am at work or on vacation, I don't respond. Most paid departments, however, work what is called a 24/48—24 hours on and then 48 hours off. This is a great shift to work, since every workday is a Friday.

I would advise someone who wants to begin a career as a firefighter to get a degree in fire science and also to get paramedic certification. And remember that the learning never stops—the day you think you know it all is the day you will injure yourself or someone else.

CHAPTER three

BECOMING A CANDIDATE: EDUCATION

THIS CHAPTER describes the different types of fire-related training programs available. You'll see sample courses and get information on training programs across the country. You'll also learn why it may work to your advantage to go to college and earn a degree, even if it's not directly related to firefighting.

THE GROWING need for increased education in order to land a firefighting job cannot be ignored. While the published minimum requirements listed for getting a job as a career firefighter are often a high school diploma or its equivalent, the reality is that the vast majority of successful firefighter applicants possess significantly more education than that. Many applicants have earned a fire science certificate or associate's degree and several have also obtained EMT training and certification in order to land a job in this highly competitive field.

All the firefighters interviewed for this book confirm that the trend in fire departments around the country is to require education beyond a high school diploma. A college degree sets an applicant above many of his or her peers, allows a firefighter to earn a higher salary than non-degree colleagues, and can be beneficial in the future. Many departments offer incentive pay for education. For instance, the Urbandale, Iowa, fire department provides bonus pay of $1,000 if you obtain a bachelor's degree. In addition, it is common practice to promote those with a college education first. When a firefighter retires, whether because of working a set number of years or because of an injury, a degree can translate into more employment options.

Even volunteer firefighters are facing stricter educational demands. Many states now require that volunteers meet the National Fire Protection Association's Standard 1001: Firefighter Professional Qualifications. To meet this standard, one must go through a rigorous basic training course that includes classroom and practical instruction.

Your local fire department can tell you the type of training job applicants have, as opposed to what is required, in your area. Ask if firefighter and/or EMT certification are needed to be hired as a municipal firefighter in your state. For example, in Florida, all job applicants must obtain Firefighter I and EMT certification before they can be hired by a municipal fire department.

There are several different routes to getting the firefighting training you need to compete successfully for a paid position. The following section describes the major types of training programs available for all ages and experience levels, ranging from high school to bachelor's degrees.

HIGH SCHOOL PREPARATION

If you haven't yet completed high school, you can take courses that will help you to prepare for a career as a firefighter. College-prep courses will cover most of the essential material. Basic skills, such as reading comprehension, writing, computer literacy, and mathematics and science, must be learned and reinforced. To go even further with your training, take as many of the following classes as possible:

chemistry
biology
health
auto mechanics

carpentry

drafting

blueprint reading

technical drawing

building construction

physical education (PE)

computer training

Spanish or other languages

By building a strong educational foundation while still in high school, you'll increase your chances of succeeding in the next phase of your training, whether it's a certificate, a college degree, or an on-the-job training program.

CALLING 911

Stories about the origins of 911 are as varied as the calls the emergency line receives. It is usually agreed, though, that an association of fire chiefs suggested such a line in 1957. The number was introduced in Congress in 1968. But it was not until 1999 that 911 was officially chosen as the nationwide emergency number. Even now, it is still not available to a few isolated areas of the United States and Canada.

FIRE EXPLORER AND FIRE CADET PROGRAMS

Depending on your age, you may be able to join a Fire Explorer or a fire cadet program to get valuable firefighter training and experience. Both of these programs are offered in many locations throughout the country. Most of them are for people between the ages of 14 and 21. However, age requirements vary; some cadet programs accept applicants through age 35.

Fire Explorer Program

The Boy Scouts of America, through its subsidiary Learning for Life, sponsors Fire Explorer programs in many locations nationwide. Through this program, Explorers between the ages of 14 and 21 can learn about every aspect of fire fighting by working with an affiliated fire department. In many cases, Explorers are allowed to respond to calls and ride along as observers. While Explorers are trained in fire suppression, they are not allowed to go into a burning building. Supervised Explorers perform numerous tasks on which firefighters inside the building rely.

For a listing of Fire Explorer programs across the country, log on to www.firehouse.com/links/Organizations/Fire_Explorers. You can also contact your local fire department to see if it has a Fire Explorer program you are eligible for. Here's a list of requirements for becoming an Explorer:

▶ be a citizen or live within ten miles of the city limits
▶ be between the ages of 14 and 21
▶ have no felony charges
▶ maintain a C average in school
▶ maintain a good standing in the community
▶ have a reliable source of transportation

Fire Cadet Programs

Many municipal fire departments offer cadet programs. These programs vary among departments, but most offer training to interested people between the ages of 18 and 35; some programs take cadets as young as 16, while others consider only applicants 21 or younger. Contact local fire departments to find out if they sponsor cadet programs and to inquire about eligibility requirements. Here are two programs, illustrating the range offered by individual fire departments.

High School Cadets
Some fire departments offer cadet firefighter programs for high school students. These programs are designed for 16- to 18-year-olds who wish to receive training and participate in departmental activities. Cadet members are required to have their guardian's permission to join and must maintain good academic standing in high school. Members are eligible for all training, but cannot ride in charge until they turn 18 years old. Some fire departments

recruit high school seniors under a high school work-study program. If you are still in high school, ask your guidance counselor for additional information about fire cadet programs offered through your local fire departments. You can also search the Internet using key words such as *cadet firefighter* or *fire cadet program* along with your city or state.

Seattle, Washington, offers its young people two opportunities to experience preemployment training as firefighters. Participants can take part in a ride-along program that allows them to do just that—ride along on trucks going to calls so they can observe firefighters at work. The cadets may not enter burning buildings, though. Members of both programs pay dues and buy their own equipment and uniforms. The groups meet on Saturday mornings.

The senior cadet program is open to men and women who are at least 19 years old, have a high school diploma or have passed an equivalency test (GED), and hold a Washington State driver's license. The company can be joined only during the strictly enforced annual enrollment period from August 1 to 14.

Senior cadets study subjects such as engine operations, search and rescue techniques, fire suppression, and problem solving. For information, call 206-615-1300.

The second Seattle program, Fire Cadet Company 511, gives men and women from 16 to 21 years old the chance to explore working in the fire industry. They train in such areas as hose handling, technical rescues, pump operations, and confined space rescues. They also learn about teamwork, problem solving, and discipline.

For information, call Seattle fire department headquarters at 206-386-1400.

General Cadet Programs

As we've said above, joining a fire cadet program is a good way to gain knowledge about a fire department, learn the basic skills of a firefighter, and get support, encouragement, and insight into pursuing a career in the fire service. Cadet programs are not limited to students. Many fire departments offer hands-on emergency medical training, work experience at fire stations, and training in firefighter skills for any cadets enrolled in their program. Eligible age levels vary among programs. As an example, here is a description of the Phoenix, Arizona, fire department cadet program.

Phoenix Cadet Program

Cadets receive hands-on emergency medical training, work experience at fire stations, training in firefighter skills, and volunteerism for the community. They are required to volunteer a minimum of 32 hours every three months to the fire department. This may be done in a variety of areas such as teaching CPR and helping with fire station open houses, public education events, or the service van program. Cadets are responsible for staffing the service van, which provides customer service support such as nonemergency transport for behavioral health incidents. Once on-duty, cadets notify the battalion chiefs to be placed on the roll call. Field battalion chiefs and captains supervise the on-duty staff of cadets.

To be eligible for the Phoenix fire cadet program, you must

- be at least 16 years old
- be able to volunteer 32 hours every three months
- complete an application
- go through a selection board interview
- get a background check
- have a valid Arizona driver's license and a good driving record

CERTIFICATE PROGRAMS

There are different types of certificates, awarded upon the completion of specific training programs, that will help increase your chances of landing a great job. For example, many technical schools, community colleges, and other schools offer certificate programs in fire science or fire technology. You can also seek EMT certification, CPR training, or other first-aid training. Some fire departments now require that all new firefighters have EMT certification prior to being hired. Check with the fire departments to which you're considering applying in order to find out about their specific requirements, as requirements often differ. If you need to obtain EMT certification, take a look at the book entitled *EMT Career Starter, Second Edition*, published by LearningExpress, to get the latest information about EMT requirements and to see an extensive directory of schools offering EMT training throughout the country.

Read all certificate materials carefully before you apply to any program of study. You should also speak to an instructor or guidance counselor at the school(s) you are considering, in order to find out if the fire science certificate offered is a good match for you. There may be several different certificates offered by one school that fall under the general heading of fire science, so you need to examine each certificate program carefully before enrolling. For example, some programs emphasize fire administration or fire inspection rather than firefighting. Other programs may be geared to people who are already employed as firefighters but need to obtain additional certification for a promotion or to master specialized skills.

Most certificate programs require that applicants have a high school diploma or its equivalent before beginning the certificate program. It is typical for programs to require regular attendance and an academic average of a C or higher to be eligible to receive a certificate upon completion of the course. Entrance requirements may include a physical ability exam and a medical exam. A one-year fire science certificate training program is detailed below. This program is offered at a community college in Burlington, New Jersey. County residents pay $2,106.00, out-of-county state residents pay $2,538.00, while nonresidents pay $4,293.00.

Fire Science Certificate

Course Name	Number of Credit Hours
Introduction to Fire Science	7
Fire Department Organization and Management	4
Fire Detection and Suppression Systems	3
Fire Service Construction Principles	4
Tactic and Strategies	3
Fire Inspection Certification	6
Total Credits	**27**

In contrast to the New Jersey program, some certificate courses offered require just one semester of study. These are usually designed for those pursuing a firefighting career as well as for those already employed in the field.

Associate Degree Programs

An associate degree program's length of study is generally either two academic years or two calendar years. Entrance requirements include a high school diploma (possibly with a college-prep course of study) or a GED. Many associate degree programs also require entrance and placement exams. An associate degree program differs from a certificate program in that some courses are taken in liberal arts along with the courses that are required for your major. Courses in your major combine classroom theory with practical application of the skills you need.

Two types of schools offer associate degree programs: community colleges and junior colleges. If you plan to live at home and work while getting your education, you might consider a community college. Community colleges are public institutions offering vocational and academic courses both during the day and at night. They typically cost less than either two- or four-year public and private institutions. Depending on your course of study, you could have one of the following when you are finished:

- ▶ an AA degree (associate in arts)
- ▶ an AS degree (associate in science)
- ▶ an AAS degree (associate in applied science)

You can locate the community colleges in your area by contacting your state's department of education. Or you can browse the web for community colleges, which are listed by state.

Junior colleges are typically more expensive than community colleges, because they tend to be privately owned. You can earn a two-year degree (AA or AS), which can usually be applied to four-year programs at most colleges and universities. Use the Internet or the best-selling guide *Peterson's Two-Year Colleges* (updated yearly) to help you with your search.

Read all college materials carefully before you apply to an associate degree program. You should also speak to an instructor or a guidance counselor at the school you are considering, in order to find out if the fire science associate's degree it offers is a good match for you. There may be several different specialties offered by one school that fall under the general heading of fire science, so you need to examine each associate degree program carefully before enrolling.

For example, some degree programs emphasize fire administration or fire protection engineering rather than firefighting. Other programs are designed for people who are already employed as firefighters and are seeking additional training to prepare for a promotion or otherwise further their career.

Some associate degree programs combine both pre-employment students and post-employment students in the same class, so you could be studying alongside several career firefighters in one or more of your courses. If that's the case, take the opportunity to get to know them and ask questions so you'll be better prepared when you enter the job-hunting phase. A community college guidance counselor from Georgia says:

> Our associate degree program is made up of both career firefighters and people who want to become career firefighters. The courses are designed so each of these two groups can benefit from them. While our program is geared more for fire lieutenants and other firefighters, we always have a number of aspiring firefighters who enroll and who benefit from the courses.

To give you an idea of what you can expect, the following chart shows associate degree training program from a community college. This is an evening program that leads to an associate in science degree in Fire Protection and Safety Technology. The total number of credit hours needed to complete the degree is 62.

Associate in Science Degree in Fire Protection and Safety Technology

Course	Credit Hours
English Composition	3
Introduction to Literature	3
Introduction to Fire Protection	3
Fundamentals of Fire Prevention	3
Hazardous Materials	3
Chemistry for Fire Service or Introduction to Chemistry	4
Fire Science Hydraulics	3
Fire Protection Systems and Equipment	3

Building Construction for the Fire Service	3
Law and the Fire Service	3
Mathematics elective	3
Humanities elective	3
Fire science electives (2)	6
Science elective	4
Introduction to Psychology	3
Introduction to Sociology	3
Social science elective	3
Electives (2)	6
Total Credits	**62**

A two-year college in New Jersey offers an associate degree in Applied Science: Fire Science Technology. It is designed for those who will seek employment as municipal public safety officers, arson investigators, industrial safety inspectors, and fire insurance and fire suppression systems salespersons, as well as firefighters. In addition to classroom instruction, this course offers the opportunity for students to develop skills in using the most advanced fire science technology.

Associate in Applied Science Degree in Fire Science Technology

Course	Credit Hours
Composition I	3
Introduction to Fire Protection	3
College Mathematics	3
Introduction to Physical Science	3
Social science elective	3
Composition II or Speech Fundamentals	3
Fundamentals of Fire Prevention	3
Fire Science course	3
Social science elective	3
Humanities electives (2)	6
Hazardous Materials I	3

Fire Protection, Building Construction	3
Fire science courses (5)	15
Electives (2)	6
Total Credits	**60**

Bachelor's Degree Programs

Colleges and universities offer undergraduate (four-year) programs in which you can earn a bachelor's degree (BA) and often a master's (MA) and a doctoral (PhD) degree in a variety of fields. Entrance requirements are more stringent than for community colleges; admissions personnel will expect you to have taken certain classes in high school to meet their admission standards. Your high school GPA and standardized test scores (most often those of the Scholastic Aptitude Tests, or SATs) will be considered. If your high school grades are weak or it has been some time since you were last in school, you might want to consider taking courses at a community college to bring you up to speed. You can always apply to the college or university as a transfer student after your academic track record has improved.

Be aware that state or public colleges and universities are generally less expensive to attend than private colleges and universities, because they receive state funds to offset their operational costs. Another thing to consider when choosing a college is its placement program in fire science. Does it have a relationship with area fire departments in which the departments actively recruit on campus and may even use the campus as the site for their training courses? Attending a school with such a relationship could greatly improve your chances of employment upon graduation.

Although many entry-level firefighters don't have a bachelor's degree, if you plan to advance in your career to the level of fire chief or want to become a fire protection engineer instead of a firefighter, a four-year degree is necessary. The following chart lists some examples of courses leading to a bachelor's degree in Fire Protection Engineering. The list does not include all the courses required for a bachelor's degree, but will give you an idea of what to expect. These courses are offered at a major university in Maryland where annual tuition per semester hour is $230 for state residents and $490 for nonresidents. Numerous fees may apply.

Fire Protection Engineer

Linear Algebra	Calculus
Differential Equations	General Physics I and II
Fire Dynamics	Mechanics of Materials
Introduction to Fire Protection Engineering	Fire Alarm and Special Hazards Design
Computer Applications	Fire Protection Fluid Mechanics
Fire Protection Systems Design I	Heat Transfer Applications in Fire Protection
Pyrometrics of Materials	Mechanics of Deformable Solids
Thermodynamics	Principles of Electrical Engineering
Fire Protection Hazard Analysis	Life Safety and Risk Analysis

Fire Academies

While many states have state-sponsored or private fire academies to train new municipal firefighters, these academies are normally for employed firefighters only. However, if a fire academy is affiliated with a community college, then prospective firefighters are normally able to enter the program. Requirements vary among states, so check carefully for fire academy entrance requirements.

IN THE NEWS

The Miami Fire-Rescue Training Center's minimum curriculum now takes 800 hours, or six months, to complete. Courses are given in areas such as firefighter standards, firefighting skills, rope rescue operations, basic water rescue, special ladders and skill drills, EMS orientation, state EMT training, and paramedic training. Once training is completed, firefighters face another five to six months of probation, during which they receive additional training.

Distance Training Programs

A growing number of programs are available that are designed for students to earn a degree in fire science at home, while working full- or part-time. Unlike community colleges, which often hold classes in the evenings and on weekends to accommodate work schedules, with distance training you never attend classes. Several colleges and universities now have programs with names like Degrees at a Distance, Correspondence Courses, or Long-Distance Learning that allow you to study and take courses on your own.

Distance learning is also known as independent study. It focuses on the idea that adults, through their jobs, personal activities, and general life experience, have many of the tools necessary to be successful independent learners. These tools include organizational and time management skills, basic writing and communication skills, and motivation and initiative. Adults also tend to make serious commitments to their education.

If you already have some work and life experience behind you and believe you are a good candidate for independent study, this could be an excellent way to get the fire service education you need. Distance learning can also be a good option for working firefighters who wish to complete their bachelor's degrees. Search the Internet with terms such as *distance learning* for schools that offer these programs. You can also find search categories under the term *education* that can help you. Also check Appendix C for books about distance learning programs.

National Fire Academy's Degrees at a Distance Program

One distance learning option for prospective firefighters is the Degrees at a Distance Program (DDP) sponsored by the National Fire Academy. It is offered by a network of accredited four-year colleges and universities that serve seven regions around the country. Course offerings are at the college junior and senior level. Through the DDP, you can take individual courses for credit to upgrade your professional skills; earn a certificate from the National Fire Academy for successfully completing six courses; or complete the entire curriculum and turn a two-year associate degree into a four-year bachelor's degree.

The DDP's course curriculum is designed to supplement each participating institution's requirements for a bachelor's degree. Like traditional college courses, these programs include reading assignments, written exercises, and exams. And just because students don't go to actual classes doesn't mean they don't have meaningful contact with qualified instructors. Most students have conferences with instructors by telephone, mail, and computer. As with traditional schooling, assignments are returned to students with detailed comments and suggestions. When it is time for exams, students travel to a central location to take them.

Learning the DDP Way

Courses offered through the Degrees at a Distance Program cover a full range of topics important to firefighters and other fire service professionals, from fire science to administration to prevention technology. Although the DDP curriculum is aimed at the junior and senior levels, its course listing is representative of the types of classes you can sign up for in traditional (nonindependent study) college programs at different academic levels:

- Fire Dynamics
- Police and Legal Foundations of Fire Protection
- The Community and Fire Threat
- Applications of Fire Research
- Incendiary Fire Analysis and Investigation
- Fire Protection Structure and Systems Design
- Fire-related Human Behavior
- Fire Prevention Organization and Management
- Analytic Approaches to Public Fire Protection
- Personnel Management for the Fire Service
- Advanced Fire Administration
- Disaster and Fire Defense Planning
- Managerial Issues in Hazardous Materials

You can contact the program's sponsor, the National Fire Academy, at the following address: National Fire Academy, Higher Education Programs, 16825 South Seton Avenue, Emmitsburg, MD 21727. You can also e-mail queries to Ed.Kaplan@fema.gov. If you wish to get information directly from participating colleges and universities, consult the list at the end of Appendix D.

HOW TO CHOOSE THE TRAINING PROGRAM THAT'S BEST FOR YOU

Because there are so many training programs, it can be a challenge to find the one that's best for you. The first step is to find out what schools near you offer fire science training or other college courses that will help you land a career firefighter job. Check the directory in Appendix D to find a list of some of the schools that offer fire-related training programs nationwide. You can also use the tips located throughout this chapter to conduct searches on the Internet.

The next step is to contact the schools for more information. You should always confirm that they currently offer courses related to fire services. Ask to speak to a guidance counselor or to someone in the fire science or fire technology department to get detailed information about the fire science programs offered. Request a school catalog and whatever brochures are available about the school and its programs. Read these documents carefully when you receive them, to find out the required courses for your program, how much it will cost, and how long the program will last.

It is worth the time to visit the schools you are interested in and talk to a guidance counselor or admissions officer at each one. These counselors are trained to help you identify your needs and decide if their school will meet them. Follow these steps when preparing for a campus visit:

1. Contact the office of admissions to request an appointment to visit. Remember to ask for the name of the person making the appointment and that of the person you will be meeting with. Try to schedule a meeting with an instructor in the fire science program as well as a guidance counselor in the admissions or counseling department.

2. Bring a copy of your transcript or permanent record card if you are meeting with an admissions officer.

3. Prepare a list of honors or awards you received in high school or the community, including documentation of any volunteer or fire cadet training.

4. Ask to tour the fire science practical experience area, if possible. This tour will show you the available equipment and materials for simulations and other fire exercises. Many schools are affiliated with

one or more local fire departments or private fire academies, so they offer this hands-on training through another agency.

5. Be prepared to ask questions about the school and the surrounding community, including extracurricular activities, work opportunities, and anything else you don't find explained in the promotional brochures.

Questions to Ask

After you visit several schools and narrow your choices down to two or three, you will need to ask tough questions about each program in order to make the final selection. You want to attend the school that will best serve your needs, help you land a job, and charge fees that you can afford (see Chapter 4 for information on securing financial aid). You may choose to apply to several programs if the admissions at your top-choice school are competitive. The following questions will assist you in determining which school is your top choice. After each question, you will find the information you need to hear for an answer.

1. Does the fire science or fire technology program admit students who are not currently full-time paid firefighters?

This is an important question to ask as a first step in evaluating a school's program. Years ago, most fire science degree programs were aimed at career firefighters who wanted to get promoted or move into a specialized area in the fire service. That has changed. Because of the competition for career firefighter positions, many more associate degree and certificate programs are available to help people gain the firefighting knowledge and experience that will set them above the crowd. Some schools advertise that they are geared to helping students learn all they can about firefighting and land a great job upon graduation. Other schools may allow only career firefighters who are working full-time at a local fire department into their program.

Depending on the requirements in your county or state, you may need to enroll in a certificate training program rather than an associate degree program in order to pass the state's examination and certification process. This is currently the standard procedure in Florida, for example. Schools also have different programs of study and different areas of specialization, such as fire protection engineering or technology, fire administration, firefighting, fire technology, and fire inspection, in addition to or under the heading of fire science.

Therefore you need to contact each school you are considering and ask to speak to an instructor or a representative of the fire science or fire technology program. Ask specifically whether you can enroll in the school's fire science program with your background and credentials, and find out what type of students the school admits to each program, to see if a certificate or an associate degree program would be best for you. Even if you can't enroll in a program as a degree-seeking student, you may be able to take selected courses on an audit basis. It doesn't hurt to ask, and any fire-related courses that you take can only improve your chances of landing your first job.

2. What requirements must be met to attend?

Entrance requirements vary. You may be required to do any one or more of the following:

- ▶ take English, math, or science placement tests
- ▶ Take and achieve a certain score on the SATs or ACT (if you have not already taken them in high school)
- ▶ submit a certain GPA from high school
- ▶ take a physical exam
- ▶ take a physical ability test

If one of the schools you are considering has an entrance requirement you might not meet, call an admissions counselor to discuss your case. Many schools offer some type of remedial help if needed so students can meet the requirement in the future.

3. What are the qualifications of the faculty?

There should be some faculty members with bachelor's or master's degrees in fire science and/or faculty members who have extensive experience as firefighters and firefighter instructors. The faculty should be accessible to students for advisory meetings and conferences to discuss class work.

4. Is the school accredited?

It's important that the school you choose be accredited. Accreditation is a rigorous and complex process that ensures sound educational and ethical business practices at the schools that achieve it. It is a process schools undergo voluntarily.

Some accrediting agencies are national and some are regional. The name of the accrediting agency for the school you're interested in will probably be plainly printed on the school's general catalog, because schools are usually proud of their accredited status. If you can't locate the information in a school's printed materials, you can make sure of their status by calling the school and asking for the name(s) of its accrediting agency or agencies.

An important point to remember is that if the school you choose is not accredited, you cannot get financial aid through any government programs. (See Chapter 4 for more information about how to obtain financial aid.)

5. Does the school have access to the latest firefighting equipment and technology?

It's a good idea, when you are visiting schools, to ask to see their fire service training equipment. Current firefighting technology and training should be available to students. The hands-on portion of the training program should cover basic firefighting principles and should offer simulation exercises to practice the basic skills needed by a firefighter, such as

▶ fire hose techniques
▶ extinguishing fires in test modules
▶ how to move while wearing heavy equipment
▶ working in smoke-filled rooms
▶ pump operations
▶ confined space rescue

6. How much will the program cost?

Tuition varies according to the length of the program, the area in which the school is located, and whether you are a resident of the state in which you are applying for school. If the tuition is not listed in the college's course catalog, call the school and ask what its current resident and nonresident rates (whichever applies to you) are. As you can see from the sample tuition costs listed earlier in the programs (certificate, associate, and bachelor's), there is quite a range of costs for completing a training program.

Don't forget to include the following items when figuring out how much each school will cost:

▶ books and supplies

▶ admission fees

▶ lab fees

▶ miscellaneous fees (parking, other mandatory fees such as student activity fees for full-time students at some schools regardless of program of study, and so on)

▶ room and board or rent

▶ transportation

▶ childcare (if required)

▶ loan origination fees (if applicable)

▶ personal expenses

After you create an estimate of the total costs for each school you are considering, you'll be armed with one more item that can make or break a school's desirability for you.

7. What is the student-teacher ratio?

The student-teacher ratio is a statistic that shows the average number of students assigned to one teacher in a classroom or lab. It's important that the student-teacher ratio not be too high. Education suffers if classrooms are too crowded or if a teacher has too many students to be able to see everyone who wishes to be seen for a private conference. According to one of the top national accrediting agencies, the Accrediting Council for Independent Colleges and Schools (ACICS), a reasonable student-teacher ratio for skills training is 30 students to one teacher in a lecture setting and 15 students to one teacher in a laboratory or clinical instruction setting. At very good schools the ratio is even better than the ACICS recommends.

8. When are classes scheduled?

If you need to work full- or part-time during regular business hours while attending school, you'll need to find a school that offers classes at nontraditional times, such as evenings or weekends.

9. Is the campus environment suitable?

When you visit the school, determine how the campus feels to you. Is it too big? Too small? Too quiet? Is the campus in a city or a rural community? Is it easily accessible? Do you need to rely on public transportation to get there? Select a school that has a campus environment that meets your needs.

10. Does the school offer childcare facilities?

If this is of concern to you, you'll want to tour the childcare facilities and interview the people who work there to see whether the care is suitable for your children.

Application Tips from Admissions Directors

- Apply as early as you can. You'll need to fill out an application and submit high school or GED transcripts and any copies of SAT, ACT, or other test scores used for admission. If you haven't taken these tests, you may have to before you can be admitted. Call the school and find out when the next program starts, then apply at least a month or two before, to make sure you can complete requirements before the program begins.
- You may receive a prewritten request for high school transcripts from the admissions office when you get your application. Forward the request quickly, so the admissions process is not held up in any way.
- Make an appointment as soon as possible to take any placement tests that may be required.
- Pay your fees before the deadline. Enrollment is not complete each quarter or semester until students have paid all fees by the date specified on the registration form. If the fees are not paid by the deadline, their class registration may be canceled. If you are hoping to receive financial aid, apply as early as you can.
- Find out early in the application process whether you must pass a physical or have any other medical history forms on file for the school you choose.

INSIDE TRACK

Ken Hendrix
Captain
Dallas Fire Department

My interest in the fire service derives from the fact that my father was in the department, and during my visits to the fire station one of the main things I noticed was the quality of the people—they all seemed like good guys, the kind of people you would want to be around. I have generally found this to be true over the course of my career. It was during my second year of college that I began to seriously look at the fire service as a career, and I was 22 years old when I became a member of the department. That was more than 30 years ago, and even back then there was so much competition that it took me two-and-a-half years to get hired. Nowadays many fire departments have a huge volume of applicants, sometimes in the hundreds, so it can take a lot of personal commitment to get the job you want.

The fire service is a tremendously challenging and rewarding career. There is nothing like the feeling you get from being able to put a good stop on a fire or being able to make a difference in someone's life in a time of crisis. One thing about the job that really keeps it interesting for me is that you never know what is going to happen next. Another benefit is that your advancement is largely determined by your own initiative, skills, and willingness to apply yourself. It is the type of career where a lot of what you get out of it depends on what you put into it. I enjoy the fact that I am in a career where even after 30 years I still look forward to going to work.

Our work schedule is 24 hours on duty and 48 hours off. There are routine daily activities at the station such as equipment readiness checks, inventory, station maintenance, and company training, among others. In addition we are involved in building inspections, hydrant maintenance, smoke detector installations, and other public service activities. The activities we are most often involved in are training, equipment readiness, and inspections.

The fire service has changed significantly over the years, especially in terms of the expansion of the scope of services we provide to the public. The fields of EMS, HAZMAT, and specialized rescue have become more prevalent in the fire service since I began my career. Recently the fire service has begun to take on more of the responsibility for responding to the threats posed by weapons of mass destruction, including chemical, biological, and nuclear incidents.

For someone considering the fire service as a profession, my advice would be to learn as much as possible about the organization you are attempting to join and to understand the scope of the services they deliver. A lot of departments provide EMS service as well as fire suppression. The EMS aspect can be very challenging and is often the bulk of the service delivery, especially in those departments where firefighters serve as paramedics as well. EMS places its own set of physical and mental demands on an individual in addition to the rigors of performing the duties necessary to being an effective firefighter. Make sure you fully understand the responsibilities of the job and are prepared to make the commitment necessary to meet the challenges and demands that you will face.

CHAPTER four

BECOMING A CANDIDATE: FINANCIAL AID

THIS CHAPTER explains the three types of financial aid available: scholarships and grants, loans, and work-study programs. You'll find out how to determine your eligibility, which financial records you'll need to gather, and how to complete and file forms (a sample financial aid form is included). At the end of the chapter are listed many more resources that can help you find the aid you need.

YOU HAVE decided that you want a job in fire protection services, and you've chosen a training program. Now you need a plan for financing your training. Whether your goal is a certificate, associate's degree, or bachelor's degree, be assured that you can qualify for aid at several different types of schools, ranging from community colleges, technical colleges, and universities to vocational schools that offer short-term training programs. You can often qualify for some type of financial aid even if you're attending only part time. The financial aid you'll get may be less than in full-time programs, but it can still be worthwhile and help you pay for a portion of your fire services training.

Don't let financial aid anxiety deter you from exploring the many options you have for financing your training program. After you've read this chapter, investigate the other resources listed in it. The Internet is probably the best source for up-to-the-minute information. If you are in school or have been accepted to a school, take advantage of financial aid advisors, whose job is to address your concerns and help you fill out the necessary paperwork.

SOME MYTHS ABOUT FINANCIAL AID

The subject of financial aid is often misunderstood. Here are three of the most common myths.

Myth #1: *Finding sources and applying for financial aid is confusing.*
Fact: The financial aid process is a set of steps that are ordered and logical. Several sources of help are available. To start with, read this chapter carefully to get a helpful overview of the entire process and suggestions on how to get the most financial aid possible. Then use one or more of the resources listed within and at the end of this chapter for additional help. If you believe you'll be able to cope with college, you'll be able to cope with looking for the money to finance your education.

Myth #2: *For most students, financial aid means getting a loan and going into heavy debt, or working while in school.*
Fact: The federal government and individual schools award grants and scholarships, which students don't have to pay back. It is also possible to receive a combination of scholarships and loans. It's worth taking out a loan if it means attending the school you really want to attend, rather than settling for your second choice or not going to school at all. It is a challenge to hold down a job while in school. However, a small amount of work-study employment (10–12 hours per week) has been shown to improve academic performance because it teaches students important time-management skills.

Myth #3: *Many unfamiliar terms and strange acronyms are used in the financial aid process.*
Fact: The process does use many acronyms and unfamiliar terms. Refer to the list of financial aid acronyms and the glossary of financial aid terms at the end of this chapter for quick definitions and clear explanations.

TYPES OF FINANCIAL AID

There are three categories of financial aid:

1. grants and scholarships—aid that you don't have to pay back
2. work-study—aid that you earn by working
3. loans—aid that you have to pay back

Grants

Grants are normally awarded based on financial need. The two most common grants are described in the following paragraphs.

Federal Pell Grants

Federal Pell Grants are based on financial need and are awarded only to undergraduate students who have not yet earned a bachelor's or professional degree. For many students, Pell Grants provide a foundation of financial aid to which other aid may be added. For the year 2008–2009, the maximum award was $4,751. You can receive only one Pell Grant in an award year, and you may not receive Pell Grant funds for more than one school at a time.

How much you get will depend not only on your expected family contribution (EFC) but also on your cost of attendance, whether you're a full-time or a part-time student, and whether you attend school for a full academic year or less. You can qualify for a Pell Grant even if you are enrolled only part-time in a training program. You should also be aware that some private and school-based sources of financial aid will not consider your eligibility if you haven't first applied for a Pell Grant.

Federal Supplemental Educational Opportunity Grants (FSEOGs)

FSEOGs are for undergraduates with exceptional financial need, that is, students with the lowest EFCs. Priority is given to students who receive Pell Grants. An FSEOG is similar to a Pell Grant in that it doesn't need to be paid back.

You can receive between $100 and $4,000 a year, depending on when you apply, your level of need, and the funding level of the school you're attending.

There's no guarantee that every eligible student will be able to receive an FSEOG. Students at each school are paid based on the availability of funds at that school, and not all schools participate in this program. To have the best chances of getting this grant, apply as early as you can after January 1 of the year in which you plan to attend school.

Scholarships

Scholarships are almost always awarded for academic merit or for special characteristics (for example, ethnic heritage, interests, sports, parents' careers, college major, and geographic location) rather than financial need. As with grants, you do not pay back your award money. Scholarships may be offered from federal, state, school, and private sources.

The best way to find scholarship money is to use one of the free search tools available on the Internet. After entering the appropriate information about yourself, a search takes place that ends with a list of those prizes for which you are eligible. Try www.fastasp.org, which bills itself as the world's largest and oldest private-sector scholarship database. Other good sites for conducting searches are www.collegescholarships.com and www.gripvision.com. If you don't have easy access to the Internet or want to expand your search, your high school guidance counselors or college financial aid officers also have plenty of information about available scholarship money.

To find private sources of aid, spend a few hours in the library looking at scholarship and fellowship books or consider a reasonably priced (under $30) scholarship search service. Use caution when dealing with scholarship search services. While most are perfectly legitimate, some scams have been reported. If you're unsure, contact a financial aid officer. See the resources section at the end of this chapter to find contact information for search services and scholarship book titles. Another place to check is in fire service magazines. If you're currently employed, find out whether your employer has funds available for education. If you're a dependent student, ask your parents and other relatives to check with groups or organizations they belong to for possible aid sources. Consider these popular sources of scholarship money:

▶ religious organizations
▶ fraternal organizations
▶ clubs, such as Rotary, Kiwanis, American Legion, or 4H
▶ athletic clubs
▶ veterans groups
▶ ethnic group associations
▶ unions

If you already know which school you will attend, check with a financial aid administrator (FAA) in the financial aid department to find out if you qualify for any institutional scholarships or other aid. Many schools offer merit-based aid for students with a high school GPA of a certain level or with a certain level of SAT scores, in order to attract more students to their school. The National Merit Scholarship Corporation awards 5,000 students annually a scholarship based solely on outstanding academic performance. Check with the fire science department to see whether it maintains a bulletin board or other method of posting available scholarships specific to fire science programs.

While you are looking for sources of scholarships, continue to enhance your chances of winning one by participating in extracurricular events and volunteer activities. You should also obtain references from people who know you well and are leaders in the community, so you can submit their names and/or letters with your scholarship applications. Make a list of any awards you've received in the past or other honors that you could list on your scholarship application.

Thousands of scholarships are awarded to students planning to enter the fire community. Some examples follow. More information about these scholarships can be found at www.umuc.edu/studserv/finaid.html. To find more sources, search the Internet with terms such as *firefighting* and *scholarship*.

Yvorra Leadership Development Scholarship Foundation

The Yvorra Leadership Development Foundation offers scholarships to members of emergency service organizations. These include volunteer, part-paid, and career personnel from fire departments, rescue squads, and emergency medical services. Contact the foundation at yld@chesapeake.net or 410-586-0500.

International Association of Arson Investigators (IAAI)

The IAAI offers scholarships of $1,000 for undergraduate students enrolled in fire science programs at two- and four-year institutions. The student must be a member of IAAI or sponsored by a member. Write to The John Charles Wilson Scholarship Fund at 2151 Priest Bridge Drive, Suite 25, Crofton, MD 21114.

Maryland State Scholarship Administration

Maryland residents who are pursuing a degree in firefighting or other safety majors at a Maryland school and who agree to serve in Maryland as firefighters or rescue squad members for a certain amount of time after graduation may be eligible for a scholarship from the Maryland State Higher Education Commission. Contact the Maryland State Higher Education Commission, 839 Bestgate Rd., Suite 400, Office of Student Financial Assistance, Annapolis, MD 21401, for more information.

Texas Higher Education Coordinating Board

Applicants must be firefighters enrolled in a fire science degree program. The scholarship award is an exemption from tuition at public colleges or universities in Texas. Call 512-427-6101 or go to grantinfo@thecb.state.tx.us.

The U.S. government offers some tax relief for education. One program that benefits mainly middle-class students is the Hope Scholarship Credit. Eligible taxpayers may claim a credit for tuition and fees up to a maximum of $1,650 per student. The credit applies only to the first two years of postsecondary education, and students must be enrolled at least half-time. To find out more about the Hope Scholarship Credit and other education credits, log on to www.irs.gov/publications/p970.

Work-Study Programs

When applying to a college or university, you can indicate that you are interested in a work-study program. You'll then be given details about the types of jobs offered in various programs—which range from giving tours of the campus to prospective students to working in the cafeteria, or shelving library books—and how much they pay.

It is also possible to get money for college by first securing a job with a fire department that agrees to cover all or part of your educational expenses. Many departments offer a tuition reimbursement program, which pays for all or part of your education. Some departments will pay only for classes related to your job. What qualifies as a job-related course may be defined in a detailed formal policy, or you may have to get your classes approved on a case-by-case basis. Fire departments that offer this benefit include those in Columbus, Ohio; Detroit, Michigan; Fort Worth, Texas; Memphis, Tennesse; and Miami and Orlando, Florida.

Some departments make it even easier to attend college by permitting supervisors to adjust your work shifts and schedules so that you can attend classes. Others offer financial incentives not only for college classes, but also for advanced state certification courses and certain in-service training programs.

You may also want to investigate the Federal Work-Study (FWS) program, which can be applied for on the Free Application for Federal Student Aid, or FAFSA. The FWS program provides jobs for undergraduate and graduate students with financial need, allowing them to earn money to help pay education expenses. It encourages community service work and provides hands-on experience related to your course of study when available. The amount of the FWS award depends on

▶ when you apply (again, apply early)
▶ your level of need
▶ the funds available at your particular school

FWS salaries are the current federal minimum wage or higher, depending on the type of work and skills required. As an undergraduate, you'll be paid by the hour (a graduate student may receive a salary), and you will receive the money directly from your school; you cannot be paid by commission or fee. The awards are not transferable from year to year, and you will need to check with the schools to which you're applying to find out if the program is available; not all schools have work-study programs in every area of study.

An advantage of working under the FWS program is that your earnings are exempt from FICA (Federal Insurance Contribution Act) taxes if you are enrolled full-time and are working less than half time. You will be assigned a job on campus, in a private nonprofit organization, or with a public agency that offers a public service. You might provide a community service relating to fire or other emergency service if your school has such a program. Some schools have agreements with private for-profit companies whose work demands fire or other emergency skills. The total hourly wages you earn in each year cannot exceed your total FWS award for that academic year and you cannot work more than 20 hours per week. Your financial aid administrator or the direct employer must consider your class schedule and your academic progress before assigning you a job.

MORE HELP FROM FIREFIGHTERS

Every year, firefighters make significant contributions to groups such as the People's Burn Foundation, to support burn units, summer camps for children and adults, and fire prevention campaigns. Thanks to funded research, knowledge about treatment of burns has become increasingly sophisticated, so survivors have more options. And, after their treatment ends, moral support is usually strong and untiring.

Student Loans

Although scholarships and grants and even work-study programs can help offset the costs of higher education, they usually don't give you enough money to pay your way entirely. Most students who can't afford to pay for their entire education rely at least in part on student loans. The largest single source of these loans—and for all money for students—is the federal government. Try these three sites for information about the U.S. government's educational funding programs:

www.fedmoney.org

This site explains everything from the application process (you can actually download the applications you'll need) and eligibility requirements to the different types of loans available.

www.finaid.org

Here you can find a calculator for figuring out how much money your education will cost (and how much you'll need to borrow), get instructions for filling out the necessary forms, and even find information on the various types of military aid available.

www.ed.gov/offices/OSFAP/Students

This is the federal student financial aid home page. The FAFSA can be filled out and submitted online.

You can also get excellent detailed information about different sources of federal education funding by sending for a copy of the U.S. Department of Education's publication The Student Guide. Write to the Federal Student Aid Information Center, PO Box 84, Washington, DC 20044, or call 800-4FED-AID.

Here are some of the most popular federal loan programs.

Federal Perkins Loans

A Perkins Loan has the lowest interest (currently 5%) of any loan available for both undergraduate and graduate students and is offered to students with exceptional financial need. You repay your school, which lends the money to you with government funds.

Depending on when you apply, your level of need, and the funding level of the school, you can borrow up to $4,000 for each year of undergraduate study. The total amount you can borrow as an undergraduate is $20,000.

The school pays you directly by check or credits your tuition account. You have nine months after you graduate (provided you were continuously enrolled at least half-time) to begin repayment, with up to ten years to pay off the entire loan.

Federal PLUS Loans (Parent Loans for Undergraduate Students)

PLUS loans enable parents with good credit histories to borrow money to pay the educational expenses of a child who is a dependent undergraduate student enrolled at least half-time. Your parents must submit the completed forms to your school.

To be eligible, your parents will be required to pass a credit check. If they don't pass, they might still be able to receive a loan if they can show that extenuating circumstances exist or if someone who is able to pass the credit check agrees to cosign the loan. Your parents must also meet citizenship requirements.

The yearly limit on a PLUS Loan is equal to your cost of attendance minus any other financial aid you receive. For instance, if your cost of attendance is $6,000 and you receive $4,000 in other financial aid, your parents could borrow up to, but no more than, $2,000. The interest rate varies, but is not to exceed 9% over the life of the loan. Your parents must begin repayment while you're still in school. There is no grace period.

Federal Stafford Loans

Stafford loans are low-interest loans that are given to students who attend school at least half-time and meet other eligibility requirements. The maximum amount you can borrow is $23,000 as a dependent undergraduate student. The lender is either the U.S. Department of Education or a bank you select, depending on the loan program under which you borrow. Check with your financial aid office for details. Stafford loans fall into one of two categories:

1. **subsidized loans**, awarded on the basis of financial need
   You will not be charged any interest on these loans before you begin repayment or during authorized periods of deferment. The federal government subsidizes the interest during these periods.
2. **unsubsidized loans**, not awarded on the basis of financial need
   You'll be charged interest on an unsubsidized loan from the time it is disbursed until it is paid in full. If you allow the interest to accumulate, it will be capitalized; that is, the interest will be added to the principal amount of your loan, and additional interest will be based upon the higher amount. This will increase the amount you have to repay.

There are many borrowing limit categories to these loans, depending on whether you get an unsubsidized or a subsidized loan, which year in school you're enrolled for, how long your program of study is, and whether you're considered independent or dependent for purposes of federal aid eligibility. You can have both kinds of Stafford loans at the same time, but the total amount of money loaned at any given time cannot exceed $23,000 for dependent students and $46,000 for independent students. The interest rate varies, but should not exceed 8.25%. An origination fee for a Stafford Loan is approximately 3% or 4% of the loan, and the fee will be deducted from each loan disbursement you receive. There is a six-month grace period after graduation before you must start repaying the loan.

Loan money is also available from state governments. Here is a list of the agencies responsible for giving out such loans, with websites and e-mail addresses where available.

ALABAMA

Alabama Commission on Higher Education
100 North Union Street
PO Box 302000
Montgomery, AL 36130-2000
334-242-2276
E-mail: deborah.nettles@ache.alabama.com

ALASKA

Alaska Commission on Postsecondary
   Education
3030 Vintage Boulevard
Juneau, AK 99801-7109
800-441-2962
Fax: 907-465-5316
E-mail: alaskaadvantage.state.ak.us/forms

ARIZONA

Arizona Commission for Postsecondary
   Education
2020 North Central Avenue, Suite 550
Phoenix, AZ 85004-4503
602-258-2435
Fax: 602-258-2483
E-mail: judi@azhighered.gov

ARKANSAS

Arkansas Department of Higher Education
114 East Capitol Avenue
Little Rock, AR 72201
501-371-2050 (Little Rock)
800-54-STUDY
E-mail: finaid@adhe.edu

CALIFORNIA

California Student Aid Commission
PO Box 419026
Rancho Cordova, CA 95741-9026
888-224-7268
Fax: 916-526-8002
E-mail: studentsupport@csac.ca.gov

COLORADO

Colorado Commission on Higher Education
Colorado Heritage Center
1380 Lawrence Street, Suite 1200
Denver, CO 80204
www.state.co.us

CONNECTICUT

Connecticut Department of Higher Education

61 Woodland Street

Hartford, CT 06105-2326

800-842-0229

Fax: 860-947-1311

E-mail: info@ctdhe.org

DELAWARE

Delaware Higher Education Commission

Carvel State Office Building, Fifth Floor

820 North French Street

Wilmington, DE 19801

302-577-3240 or 800-292-7935

Fax: 302-577-6765

E-mail: dhec@doe.K12.de.us

DISTRICT OF COLUMBIA

Office of the State Superintendent of
Education

441 Fourth Street, NW, Suite 350 North

Washington, DC 20001

202-727-6436 or 877-485-6751

Fax: 202-727-2834

E-mail: osse@dc.gov

www.osse.dc.gov

FLORIDA

Florida Department of Education

Office of Student Financial Assistance

325 West Gaines Street

Tallahassee, FL 32399-0400

888-827-2004

Fax: 850-488-3612

E-mail: osfa@fldoe.org

www.floridastudentfinancialaid.org

GEORGIA

Georgia Student Finance Commission

2082 East Exchange Place, Suite 100

Tucker, GA 30084

770-724-9030 or 800-505-4732

Email: info@gsfc.org

www.gsfc.org

HAWAII

Hawaii State Postsecondary Education
Commission

2444 Dole Street, Room 109J

Honolulu, HI 96822-2394

808-956-6624

Fax: 808-956-0798

Email: ckawasak@hawaii.edu

IDAHO

Idaho State Board of Education

PO Box 83720

Boise, ID 83720-0037

208-334-2270

Fax: 208-334-2632

Email: board@osbe.idaho.gov

ILLINOIS

Illinois Student Assistance Commission (ISAC)

1755 Lake Cook Road

Deerfield, IL 60015-5209

800-899-4722

Email: collegezone@isac.org

www.isac-online.org

INDIANA

State Student Assistance Commission of
   Indiana
150 West Market Street, Suite 500
Indianapolis, IN 46204-2811
317-232-2350
-or-
(for IN residents only) 888-528-4719
Fax: 317-232-3260
Email: grants@ssaci.state.in.us

IOWA

Iowa College Student Aid Commission
200 10th Street, Fourth Floor
Des Moines, IA 50309-3609
515-281-3501
-or-
(for IA residents only) 800-383-4222
E-mail: csac@max.state.ia.us
www.iowacollegeaid.org

KANSAS

Board of Regents
Curtis State Office Building
1000 SW Jackson Street, Suite 520
Topeka, KS 66612-1368
785-296-3421
Fax: 785-296-0983
E-mail: Christy@kbor.state.ks.us
www.ukans.edu/~kbor

KENTUCKY

Kentucky Higher Education Assistance
   Authority (KHEAA)
PO Box 798
Frankfort, KY 40602
800-928-8926
Fax: 502-696-7345
E-mail: webmaster@kheaa.com
www.kheaa.com

LOUISIANA

Louisiana Office of Student Financial
   Assistance
PO Box 91202
Baton Rouge, LA 70821-9202
800-259-5626 ext 1012
-or-
225-922-1012
Fax: 225-922-1089
E-mail (for students):
custserv@osfa.state.la.us
-or-
webmaster@osfa.state.la.us
www.osfa.state.la.us

MAINE

Finance Authority of Maine
3 Community Drive
Augusta, ME 04332-0949
800-228-3734
-or-
207-623-3263
Fax: 207-623-0095
E-mail: info@famemaine.com

MARYLAND

Maryland Higher Education Commission

Office of Student Financial Assistance

839 Bestgate Road, Suite 400

Annapolis, MD 21401

800-974-1024

Email: osfamail@mhec.state.md.us

MASSACHUSETTS

Massachusetts Board of Higher Education

Office of Student Financial Assistance

454 Broadway, Suite 200

Revere, MA 02151

617-727-9420

Fax: 617-727-0667

Email: osfa@mass.edu

MICHIGAN

Student Financial Services Bureau

PO Box 30047

Lansing, MI 48909-7547

800-642-5626 x 37054

Fax: 517-241-0155

E-mail: sfs@michigan.gov

www.michigan.gov/studentaid

MINNESOTA

Minnesota Higher Education Services Office

1450 Energy Park Drive, Suite 350

St. Paul, MN 55108-5227

800-657-3866

-or-

651-259-3901

E-mail: one@state.mn.us

www.mheso.state.mn.us

MISSISSIPPI

Mississippi Postsecondary Education

Financial Assistance Board

3825 Ridgewood Road

Jackson, MS 39211-6453

601-432-6647

-or-

(for MS residents only) 800-327-2980

Fax: 601-982-6527

E-mail: commissioner@ihl.state.ms.us

MISSOURI

Missouri Department of Higher Education

3515 Amazonas Drive

Jefferson City, MO 65109-5717

800-473-6757

-or-

573-751-2361

Fax: 573-751-6635

www.mocbhe.gov

Email: info@dhe.mo.gov

MONTANA

Montana University System

46 North Last Chance Gulch

PO Box 203201

Helena, MT 59620-3201

406-444-6570

E-mail: scholars@mgslp.state.mt.us

www.mgslp.state.mt.us

NEBRASKA

Coordinating Commission for Postsecondary
  Education
140 N. Eighth Street, Suite 300
PO Box 95005
Lincoln, NE 68509-5005
402-471-2847
Fax: 402-471-2886
www.ccpe.state.ne.us

NEVADA

Nevada Department of Education
700 East Fifth Street
Carson City, NV 89701-5096
775-687-9200
Fax: 775-687-9101
http://system.nevada.edu

NEW HAMPSHIRE

Postsecondary Education Commission
3 Barrell Court
Concord, NH 03301-8512
603-271-2555
Fax: 603-271-2696
www.state.nh.us

NEW JERSEY

Higher Education Student Assistance
  Authority
4 Quakerbridge Plaza
PO Box 540
Trenton, NJ 08625
800-792-8670
Fax: 609-588-7389
www.state.nj.us/treasury/osa

NEW MEXICO

New Mexico Higher Education Department
1068 Cerrillos Road
Santa Fe, NM 87505
800-279-9777
Fax: 505-476-6511
E-mail: highered@che.state.nm.us
www.hed.state.nm.us

NEW YORK

New York State Higher Education Services
  Corporation
79 Washington Avenue
Albany, NY 12255
888-697-4372 or 518-473-1574
Fax: 518-474-2839
www.hesc.org

NORTH CAROLINA

North Carolina State Education Assistance
  Authority
PO Box 13663
Research Triangle Park, NC 27709-3663
919-549-8614
-or-
(for NC residents only) 800-700-1775
E-mail: information@ncseaa.edu
www.cfnc.org

NORTH DAKOTA

North Dakota University System

North Dakota Student Financial Assistance
   Program

600 East Boulevard Avenue, Dept. 215

Bismarck, ND 58505-0230

701-328-4114

Fax: 701-328-2961

E-mail: indus.office@indus.nodak.edu

www.indus.org

OHIO

Ohio Board of Regents

PO Box 182452

Columbus, OH 43218-2452

888-833-1133

Fax: 614-752-5903

www.regents.ohio.gov

OKLAHOMA

State Regents for Higher Education

655 Research Parkway, Suite 200

Oklahoma City, OK 73104

405-225-9100

-or-

800-858-1840

Fax: 405-225-9230

www.okhighered.org

OREGON

Oregon State Scholarship Commission

1500 Valley River Drive, Suite 100

Eugene, OR 97401-2130

800-452-8807

Fax 541-687-7419

E-mail:

public_information@mercury.osac.state.or.us

www.ossc.state.or.us

PENNSYLVANIA

Pennsylvania Higher Education Assistance
   Authority

1200 North Seventh Street

Harrisburg, PA 17102-1444

717-720-280

-or-

(for PA residents only) 800-692-7435

www.pheaa.org

RHODE ISLAND

Rhode Island Higher Education Assistance
   Authority

560 Jefferson Boulevard

Warwick, RI 02886

401-736-1100

-or-

800-922-9855

Fax: 401-732-3541

E-mail: info@riheaa.org

www.riheaa.org

SOUTH CAROLINA

South Carolina Higher Education Tuition
   Grants Commission

1333 Main Street, Suite 200

Columbia, SC 29201

803-737-2260

Fax: 803-737-2297

Website: www.state.sc.us/tuitiongrants

SOUTH DAKOTA

Board of Regents

306 East Capitol Avenue, Suite 200

Pierre, SD 57501-2545

605-773-3455

Fax: 605-773-5320

E-mail: info@sdbor.edu

www.sdbor.edu

TENNESSEE

Tennessee Student Assistance Corporation

404 James Robertson Parkway, Suite 1900

Nashville, TN 37243

615-741-1346

Fax: 615-741-6230

www.state.tn.us/tsac

TEXAS

Texas Higher Education Coordinating Board

PO Box 12788, Capitol Station

Austin, TX 78711

800-242-3062

-or-

512-427-6101

Fax: 512-427-6127

E-mail: grantinfo@thecb.state.tx.us

UTAH

Gateway Center

60 South 400 West

Salt Lake City, UT 84101-1284

801-321-7103

Fax: 801-321-7156

www.utahsbr.edu

VERMONT

Vermont Student Assistance Corporation

10 East Allen Street

PO Box 2000

Winooski, VT 05404-2601

800-642-3177

-or-

802-655-9602

Fax: 802-654-3765

E-mail: info@vsac.org

www.vsac.org

VIRGINIA

State Council of Higher Education

James Monroe Building, Ninth Floor

101 North Fourteenth Street

Richmond, VA 23219-3684

804-225-2600

Fax: 804-225-2604

www.scher.edu

WASHINGTON

Washington State Higher Education
   Coordinating Board

PO Box 43430

917 Lakeridge Way

Olympia, WA 98504-3430

360-753-7800

Fax: 360-753-7808

E-mail: info@hecb.wa.gov

www.hecb.wa.gov

WEST VIRGINIA

Higher Education Policy Commission

1018 Kanawha Boulevard East, Suite 700

Charleston, WV 25301-2827

304-558-0699

Fax: 304-558-1011

http://wvhepcnew.wvnet.edu

WISCONSIN

Wisconsin Higher Education Aids Board

131 West Wilson Street, Suite 902

Madison, WI 53703

608-267-2206

Fax: 608-267-2808

WYOMING

Wyoming Community College Commission

2020 Carey Avenue, Eighth Floor

Cheyenne, WY 82002

307-777-7763

Fax 307-777-6567

www.commission.wcc.edu

QUESTIONS TO ASK BEFORE YOU TAKE OUT A LOAN

In order to get the facts regarding the loan you're about to take out, ask the following questions:

1. *What is the interest rate and how often is the interest capitalized?* Your college's financial aid administrator will be able to tell you this.

2. *What fees will be charged?* Government loans generally have an origination fee, which goes to the federal government or the bank, depending on the loan program, to help offset its costs, and a guarantee fee, which goes to a guaranty agency for insuring the loan. Both are deducted from the amount given to you.

3. *Will I have to make any payments while still in school?* Usually you won't and, depending on the type of loan, the government may even pay the interest for you while you're in school.

4. *What is the grace period, the period after my schooling ends, during which no payment is required? Is the grace period long enough, realistically, for me to find a job and get on my feet?* A six-month grace period is common.

5. *When will my first payment be due, and approximately how much will it be?* You can get a good preview of the repayment process from the answer to this question.

6. *Who exactly will hold my loan? To whom will I be sending payments? Whom should I contact with questions or inform of changes in my situation?* Your loan may be sold by the original lender to a secondary market institution, in which case you will be notified as to the contact information for your new lender.

7. *Will I have the right to prepay the loan, without penalty, at any time?* Some loan programs allow prepayment with no penalty but others do not.

8. *Will deferments and forbearances be possible if I am temporarily unable to make payments?* You need to find out how to apply for a deferment or forbearance if you need it.

9. *Will the loan be canceled (forgiven) if I become totally and permanently disabled or if I die?* This is always a good option to have on any loan you take out.

APPLYING FOR FINANCIAL AID

Now that you're aware of the types of aid available, you'll want to begin applying as soon as possible. You've heard about the FAFSA many times in this chapter already and have an idea of its importance. This is the form used by federal and state governments, as well as school and private funding sources, to determine your eligibility for grants, scholarships, and loans. The easiest way to get a copy is to log onto www.ed.gov/offices/OSFAP/students, where you can also find help in completing the form; you can then submit the completed form electronically. You can also get a copy by calling 800-4-FED-AID or stopping by your public library or your school's financial aid office. Be sure to get an original form, because photocopies of federal forms are not accepted.

The second step of the process is to create a financial aid calendar. Using any standard calendar, write in all of the application deadlines for each step of the financial aid process. You will be able to see at a glance what needs to be done when. Start this calendar by writing in the date you requested your FAFSA. Then mark down when you received it and when you sent in the completed form. Add important dates and deadlines for any other applications you need to complete for school-based or private aid as you progress though the financial aid process. Using and maintaining a calendar will help the whole financial aid process run more smoothly and give you peace of mind that the important dates are not forgotten.

JUST THE FACTS

Smoke jumpers wear approximately 80 pounds of equipment when they jump from a plane, including a padded Kevlar jumpsuit and helmet with a metal face grate. Each pair of jumpers gets a fire box, which is dropped by parachute and contains tools, food, and water to support them for up to 48 hours.

When to Apply

Apply for financial aid as soon as possible after January 1 of the year in which you want to enroll in school. For example, if you want to begin school in the fall of 2009, then you should apply for financial aid as soon as possible after January 1, 2009. It is easier to complete the FAFSA after you have completed your tax return, so you may want to consider filing your taxes as early as possible as well. You can complete the FAFSA with estimated information and correct it after taxes are filed, so don't use incomplete tax returns as an excuse not to do the FAFSA early—it only hurts your chances of receiving maximum aid. Do not sign, date, or send your application before January 1 of the year for which you are seeking aid. If you apply by mail, send your completed application in the envelope that came with the original application. The envelope is already addressed, and using it insures that your application reaches the correct address. Do not send the FAFSA by FedEx, UPS, or other overnight mail, as it will not get there (the FAFSA is sent to a post office box). You can apply over the Internet; contact the Department of Education online (see p. 115) for details.

Many students lose out on thousands of dollars in grants and loans because they file their applications too late. A financial aid administrator from New Jersey says:

> When you fill out the Free Application for Federal Student Aid (FAFSA), you are applying for all aid available, both federal and state, work-study, student loans, et cetera. The important thing is complying with the deadline date. Those students who do are considered for the Pell Grant, the SEOG (Supplemental Educational Opportunity Grant), and the Perkins Loan, which is the best loan as far as interest goes. Lots of students miss the June 30th deadline, and it can mean losing $2,480 from TAG, and another $1,100 from EOF. Students, usually the ones who need the money most, often ignore the deadlines.

After you mail in your completed FAFSA, your application will be processed in approximately four weeks. Then you will receive a Student Aid Report (SAR) in the mail. The SAR will disclose your expected family contribution (EFC), the number used to determine your eligibility for federal student aid. Each school you list on the application may also receive your application information if the school is set up to receive it electronically.

You must reapply for financial aid every year. However, after your first year, you will receive an SAR in the mail before the application deadline. If no corrections need to be made, you can just sign it and send it in.

Getting Your Forms Filed

Follow these three simple steps if you are not completing and submitting the FAFSA online:

1. Get an original Federal Application for Federal Student Aid (FAFSA). Remember to pick up an original copy of this form, as photocopies are not acceptable.
2. Fill out the entire FAFSA as completely as possible. Make an appointment with a financial aid counselor if you need help. Read the form completely, and don't skip any relevant portions.
3. Return the FAFSA before the deadline date. Financial aid counselors warn that many students don't file the forms before the deadline and thus lose out on available aid. Don't be one of those students!

Financial Need

Financial aid from many of the programs discussed in this chapter is awarded on the basis of need (the exceptions include unsubsidized Stafford, PLUS, and consolidation loans, and some scholarships and grants). When you apply for federal student aid by completing the FAFSA, the information you report is used in a formula established by the U.S. Congress. The formula determines your EFC, the amount you and your family are expected to contribute toward your education. If your EFC is below a certain amount, you'll be eligible for a Pell Grant, assuming you meet all other eligibility requirements.

There is no maximum EFC that defines eligibility for the other financial aid options. Instead, your EFC is used in an equation to determine your financial needs:

Cost of Attendance – EFC = Financial Need

A financial aid administrator calculates your cost of attendance and subtracts the amount you and your family are expected to contribute toward that cost. If there's anything left over, you're considered to have financial need.

Are You Considered Dependent or Independent?

Federal policy uses strict and specific criteria to determine whether a student is dependent or independent and those criteria apply equally to all applicants for federal student aid. A dependent student is expected to have a parental contribution to school expenses, and an independent student is not. The parental contribution depends on the number of parents with earned income, their total income and assets, the age of the older parent, the family size, and the number of family members enrolled in postsecondary schools. Income is not just the adjusted gross income from the tax return, but also includes nontaxable income such as social security benefits and child support.

You're an independent student if *at least one* of the following applies to you:

▶ You are 24 years of age.
▶ You are married (even if you are separated).
▶ You have legal dependents other than a spouse who get more than half of their support from you and will continue to get that support during the award year.
▶ You are an orphan or ward of the court (or were a ward of the court until age 18).
▶ You are a graduate or professional student.
▶ You are a veteran of the U.S. Armed Forces, formerly engaged in active service in the U.S. Army, Navy, Air Force, Marines, or Coast Guard or as a cadet or midshipman at one of the service academies and released under a condition other than dishonorable discharge. (ROTC students, members of the National Guard, and most reservists are not considered veterans, nor are cadets and midshipmen still enrolled in one of the military service academies.)
▶ You have special and unusual circumstances that can be documented to your college financial aid administrators (for example, abuse in the family, alcoholism, and so on). This is extremely rare, and only an experienced financial aid administrator at your college can make this

dependency override on the FAFSA application. Denial of an override request cannot be appealed to the Department of Education. The financial aid administrator's decision is final.

If you live with your parents and if they claimed you as a dependent on their last tax return, then your need will be based on your parents' income. You do not qualify for independent status just because your parents have decided not to claim you as an exemption on their tax return (this used to be the case but is no longer) or do not want to provide financial support for your college education.

Students are classified as dependent or independent because federal student aid programs are based on the idea that students (and their parents or spouse, if applicable) have the primary responsibility for paying for their postsecondary education.

Gathering Financial Records

Your financial need for most grants and loans depends on your financial situation. Once you've determined whether you are considered a dependent or an independent student, you'll know whose financial records you need to gather for this step of the process. If you are a dependent student, then you must gather not only your own financial records, but also those of your parents, because you must report their income and assets as well as your own when you complete the FAFSA. If you are an independent student, then you need to gather only your own financial records (and those of your spouse if you're married). Gather your tax records from the year prior to the one in which you are applying. For example, if you are applying for financial aid for the fall of 2009, you will use your tax records from the year 2008.

To help you fill out the FAFSA, gather the following documents:

- U.S. income tax returns (IRS Form 1040, 1040A, or 1040EZ) for the year that just ended and corresponding W-2 and 1099 forms
- records of untaxed income, such as social security benefits, AFDC (Aid to Families with Dependent Children) or ADC (Aid to Dependent Children) payments, child support, welfare, pensions, military subsistence allowances, and veteran's benefits

- current bank statements and mortgage information
- medical and dental expenses for the past year that weren't covered by health insurance
- business and/or farm records
- records of investments, such as stocks, bonds, and mutual funds, as well as bank certificates of deposit (CDs) and recent statements from money market accounts
- social security number(s)

Even if you do not complete your federal income tax return until March or April, you should not wait to file your FAFSA until your tax returns are filed with the IRS. Instead, use estimated income information and submit the FAFSA, as noted earlier, just as soon as possible after January 1. Be as accurate as possible, knowing that you can correct estimates later.

GENERAL GUIDELINES FOR LOANS

Before you commit yourself to any loans, be sure to keep in mind that they will need to be repaid. Estimate realistically how much you'll earn when you leave school, remembering that you'll have other monthly obligations such as housing, food, and transportation expenses.

Once You're in School

Once you have your loan(s) and are attending classes, you should start to take responsibility for it. Keep a file of information on your loan that includes copies of all your loan documents and related correspondence, along with a record of all your payments. Open and read all your mail about your education loan.

Remember also that you are obligated by law to notify both your financial aid administrator and the holder or servicer of your loan if there is a change in your:

▶ name
▶ address

▶ enrollment status (dropping to less than half-time means that you'll have to begin payment six months later)

▶ anticipated graduation date

After You Leave School

After graduation, you must begin repaying your student loan immediately or after a stated grace period. For example, if you have a Stafford loan, you will have a six-month grace period before your first payment is due; other types of loans have grace periods as well. If you haven't been out in the world of work before, you'll begin your credit history with your loan repayment. If you make payments on time, you'll build up a good credit rating, and credit will be easier for you to obtain for other things. Get off to a good start, so you don't run the risk of going into default. If you default or refuse to pay back your loan, any number of the following things could happen to you as a result. You could

▶ have trouble getting any kind of credit in the future

▶ no longer qualify for federal or state educational financial aid

▶ have holds placed on your college records

▶ have your wages garnished

▶ have future federal income tax refunds withheld

▶ have your assets seized

You should also remember that your financial status might be examined as part of your background check when you apply to a fire department. A bad credit history could prevent you from achieving your goal of becoming a firefighter. To avoid the negative consequences of going into default in your loan, be sure to do the following:

▶ Open and read all mail you receive about your education loans immediately.

▶ Make scheduled payments on time; since interest is calculated daily, delays can be costly.

▶ Contact your loan servicer immediately if you can't make payments on time; he or she may be able to get you into a graduated or income-sensitive/income-contingent repayment plan or work with you to arrange a deferment or forbearance.

There are a few circumstances under which you won't have to repay your loan. If you become permanently and totally disabled, you probably will not have to (providing the disability did not exist prior to your obtaining the aid). Likewise, if you die, if your school closes permanently in the middle of the term, or if you are erroneously certified for aid by the financial aid office, you will not have to make payments on the loan. However, if you're simply disappointed in your program of study or don't get the job you wanted after graduation, you are not relieved of your obligation.

Loan Repayment

When it comes time to repay your loan, you will make payments to your original lender, to a secondary market institution to which your lender has sold your loan, or to a loan servicing specialist acting as its agent to collect payments. At the beginning of the process, try to choose the lender that offers you the best benefits (for example, a lender that lets you pay electronically, offers lower interest rates to those who consistently pay on time, and/or has a toll-free number to call 24 hours a day, 7 days a week). Ask the financial aid administrator at your college to direct you to such lenders.

Be sure to check out your repayment options before borrowing. Lenders are required to offer repayment plans that will make it easier to pay back your loans. Your repayment options may include

▶ **Standard repayment:** full principal and interest payments due each month throughout your loan term. You'll pay the least amount of interest using the standard repayment plan, but your monthly payments may seem high when you're just out of school.

▶ **Graduated repayment:** interest-only or partial interest monthly payments due early in repayment, with payment amounts increasing thereafter. Some lenders offer interest-only or partial interest repayment options that provide the lowest initial monthly payments available.

▶ **Income-based repayment:** monthly payments based on a percentage of your monthly income.

▶ **A consolidation loan:** several types of federal student loans with various repayment schedules consolidated into one loan. This loan is designed to help student or parent borrowers simplify their loan repayments. The interest rate on a consolidation loan may be lower than what you're currently paying on one or more of your loans. The phone number for loan consolidation at the William D. Ford Direct Loan Program is 800-557-7392. Financial administrators recommend that you do not consolidate a Perkins Loan with any other loans, since the interest on a Perkins Loan is already the lowest available. Loan consolidation is not available from all lenders.

▶ **Prepayment:** paying more than is required on your loan each month or in a lump sum. This option is allowed for all federally sponsored loans at any time during the life of the loan without penalty. Prepayment will reduce the total cost of your loan.

It's quite possible—in fact likely—that while you're still in school your FFELP (Federal Family Education Loan Program) loan will be sold to a secondary market institution such as Sallie Mae. You'll be notified of the sale by letter, and you need not worry if this happens; your loan terms and conditions will remain exactly the same, or they may even improve. Indeed, the sale may give you repayment options and benefits that you would not have had otherwise. Your payments after you finish school and your requests for information should be directed to the new loan holder.

If you receive any interest-bearing student loans, you will have to attend exit counseling after graduation, where the loan lenders will tell you the total amount of your debt and work out a payment schedule with you to determine the amounts and dates of repayment. Many loans do not become due until at least six to nine months after you graduate, giving you a grace period. For example, you do not have to begin paying on the Perkins loan until nine months after you graduate. This grace period is to give you time to find a good job and start earning money. However, during this time, you may have to pay the interest on your loan.

If for some reason you remain unemployed when your payments become due, you may receive an unemployment deferment for a certain length of time. For many loans, you will have a maximum repayment period of ten years (excluding periods of deferment and forbearance).

THE MOST FREQUENTLY ASKED QUESTIONS ABOUT FINANCIAL AID

Here are answers to the most frequently asked questions about student financial aid:

1. *I probably don't qualify for aid. Should I apply for it anyway?* Yes. Many students and families mistakenly think they don't qualify for aid and so fail to apply. Remember that there are some sources of aid that are not based on need. The FAFSA form is free—there's no good reason for not applying.
2. *Do I need to be admitted at a particular university before I can apply for financial aid?* No. You can apply for financial aid any time after January 1. However, to get the funds, you must be admitted and enrolled in school.
3. *Do I have to reapply for financial aid every year?* Yes, and if your financial circumstances change, you may get either more or less aid. After your first year, you will receive a renewal application that contains preprinted information from the previous year's FAFSA. Renewal of your aid also depends on your making satisfactory progress toward a degree and achieving a minimum GPA.
4. *Are my parents responsible for my educational loans?* No. You and you alone are responsible for your loans, unless your parents endorse or co-sign them. Parents are, however, responsible for the federal PLUS loans. If your parents (or grandparents or uncle or distant cousins) want to help pay off your loan, you can have your billing statements sent to their address.
5. *If I take a leave of absence from school, do I have to start repaying my loans?* Not immediately, but you will after the grace period. Generally, if you use your grace period up during your leave, you'll have to begin repayment immediately after graduation unless you apply for an extension of the grace period before it's used up.

6. *If I get assistance from another source, should I report it to the student financial aid office?* Yes—and, sadly, your aid amount will probably be lowered accordingly. But you'll get into trouble later on if you don't report it.

7. *Are federal work-study earnings taxable?* Yes, you must pay federal and state income tax on them, although you may be exempt from FICA taxes if you are enrolled full-time and work less than 20 hours a week.

8. *My parents are separated or divorced. Which parent is responsible for filling out the FAFSA?* If your parents are separated or divorced, the custodial parent is responsible for filling out the FAFSA. The custodial parent is the parent with whom you lived the most during the past 12 months. Note that this is not necessarily the same as the parent who has legal custody. The question of which parent must fill out the FAFSA becomes complicated in many situations, so you should take your particular circumstances to the student financial aid office for help.

Financial Aid Checklist

❏ Explore your options as soon as possible once you've decided to begin a training program.

❏ Find out what your school requires and what financial aid it offers.

❏ Complete and mail the FAFSA as soon as possible after January 1.

❏ Complete and mail other applications by their deadlines.

❏ Gather loan application information and forms from your college financial aid office.

❏ Complete the student (and parent, for PLUS loans) portion of loan applications and submit to the school for processing. Don't forget to sign the loan application.

❏ Carefully read all letters and notices from the school, the federal student aid processor, the need analysis service, and private scholarship organizations. Note whether financial aid will be sent before or after you are notified about admission, and note exactly how you will receive the money.

❏ Promptly return all documents the financial aid office requests.

❏ Report any changes in your financial resources or expenses to your financial aid office so your award can be adjusted accordingly.

❏ Reapply each year.

Financial Aid Acronyms

ADC	Aid to Dependent Children
AFDC	Aid to Families with Dependent Children
COA	Cost of Attendance
CWS	College Work-Study
EFC	Expected Family Contribution
EFT	Electronic Funds Transfer
EOF	Educational Opportunity Fund
ESAR	Electronic Student Aid Report
ETS	Educational Testing Service
FAA	Financial Aid Administrator
FAF	Financial Aid Form
FAFSA	Free Application for Federal Student Aid
FAO	Financial Aid Office
FDSLP	Federal Direct Student Loan Program
FFELP	Federal Family Education Loan Program
FICA	Federal Insurance Contributions Act
FSEOG	Federal Supplemental Educational Opportunity Grant
FWS	Federal Work-Study
GSL	Guaranteed Student Loan (now called subsidized Stafford Loan)
PC	Parent Contribution
PLUS	Parent Loan for Undergraduate Students
SAP	Satisfactory Academic Progress
SAR	Student Aid Report
SC	Student Contribution
SEOG	Supplemental Education Opportunity Grant
SLS	Supplemental Loan for Students (now called unsubsidized Stafford Loan)
TAG	Tuition Aid Grant
USED	U.S. Department of Education

GLOSSARY OF FINANCIAL AID TERMS

accrued interest. Interest that accumulates on the unpaid principal balance of a loan.

capitalization of interest. Addition of accrued interest to the principal balance of your loan that increases both your total debt and monthly payments.

default. Failure to repay a loan.

deferment. A period during which a borrower who meets certain criteria may suspend loan payments.

delinquency. Failure to make payments when due.

disbursement. Loan funds issued by the lender.

forbearance. Temporary adjustment to repayment schedule for cases of financial hardship.

grace period. The specified period of time after you graduate or leave school during which you need not make loan payments.

holder. The institution that currently owns your loan.

in-school, grace, and deferment interest subsidy. Interest the federal government pays for borrowers on some loans while the borrower is in school, during authorized deferments, and during grace periods.

interest. The cost you pay to borrow money.

interest-only payment. A payment that covers only interest owed on the loan and none of the principal balance.

lender (Originator). The organization that puts up the money when you take out a loan. Most lenders are financial institutions, but some state agencies and schools make loans too.

origination fee. A fee, deducted from the principal of a loan, that is paid to the federal government to offset the cost of the subsidy to borrowers under certain loan programs.

principal. The amount you borrow, which may increase as a result of capitalization of interest, and the amount on which you pay interest.

promissory note. A contract between you and the lender that includes all the terms and conditions under which you promise to repay your loan.

secondary markets. Institutions that buy student loans from originating lenders, thus providing lenders with funds to make new loans.

servicer. The organization that administers and collects your loan; the service may be the holder of your loan or an agent acting on its behalf.

subsidized Stafford loans. Loans based on financial need; the government pays the interest on a subsidized Stafford Loan for borrowers while they are in school and during specified deferment periods.

unsubsidized Stafford loans (formerly Supplemental Loan for Students). Loans available to borrowers regardless of family income. Unsubsidized Stafford Loan borrowers are responsible for the interest during in-school, deferment, and repayment periods.

FINANCIAL AID RESOURCES

In addition to the sources listed throughout this chapter, the following resources may be used to obtain more information about financial aid.

You should *never* pay a fee to qualify for a scholarship. For the warning signs of a scam, go to http://finaid.org.

Telephone Numbers

Federal Student Aid Information Center
(U. S. Department of Education)

Hotline	800-4-FED-AID
	-or-
	800-433-3243
TDD for the hearing-impaired	800-730-8913
Selective Service	847-688-6888
Immigration and Naturalization (INS)	800-375-5283
Internal Revenue Service (IRS)	800-829-1040
Social Security Administration	800-772-1213
National Merit Scholarship Corporation	847-866-5100
Sallie Mae (college answer service)	888-272-5543
Career College Association	202-336-6700

American College Testing (ACT)
(for information about forms
submitted to the need analysis servicer)   319-337-1000
College Scholarship Service (CSS)   732-940-8515
Need Access/Need Analysis Service   800-282-1550
FAFSA on the Web (for processing/software problems) 800-433-3243

Websites

http://studentaid.ed.gov/students/publications
The Student Guide is a free informative brochure about financial aid and is
available online at the Department of Education's website listed here.

www.fafsa.ed.gov
This site offers students help in completing the FAFSA. The site enables
you to fill out and submit the FAFSA online. You'll need to print out,
sign, and send in the release and signature pages.

www.career.org
This is the website of the Career College Association (CCA), which of-
fers a limited number of scholarships for attendance at private proprietary
schools. You can also contact the CCA at 1101 Connecticut Avenue, NW,
Suite 900, Washington, DC 20036.
E-mail: scholarships@career.org

www.salliemae.com
The Sallie Mae website contains information about loan programs.

www.collegescholarships.com
This is a fee-based service.
E-mail: staff@collegescholarships.com

www.fastweb.com
This is a scholarship database that is frequently updated.

Software Programs

Chronicle Guidance Publications
66 Aurora Street
Moravia, NY 13118-1190
800-899-0454
www.chronicleguidance.com

Peterson's Award Search
PO Box 2123
Princeton, NJ 08543-2123
888-438-2633
E-mail: custsvc@petersons.com

Books and Pamphlets

Cassidy, Daniel J. *The Scholarship Book: The Complete Guide to Private-Sector Scholarships, Fellowships, Grants, and Loans for the Undergraduate.* 13th edition. Englewood Cliffs, NJ: Prentice Hall, 2008.

Chany, Kalman A., and Geoff Martz. *Student Advantage Guide to Paying for College.* New York: Random House, The Princeton Review, 1997.

College School Service. *College Costs & Financial Aid Handbook.* 25th edition. New York: The College Board, 2006.

Cook, Melissa L. *College Student's Handbook to Financial Assistance and Planning.* Traverse City, MI: Moonbeam Publications, Inc., 1992.

Davis, Kristin. *Financing College: How to Use Savings, Financial Aid, Scholarships, and Loans to Afford the School of Your Choice.* Washington, DC: Kiplinger's Books, 2007.

Hern, Davis, and Joyce Lain Kennedy. *College Financial Aid for Dummies.* New York: IDG Books Worldwide, 1999.

How Can I Receive Financial Aid for College? Published from the Parent Brochures ACCESS ERIC Website. Order a printed copy by calling 800-LET-ERIC or write to ACCESS ERIC, Research Boulevard, MS 5F, Rockville, MD 20850-3172.

Peterson's Guides. *Peterson's Scholarships, Grants and Prizes 2008.* Princeton, NJ: Peterson's, 2007.

————. *Scholarships, Grants & Prizes: Guide to College Financial Aid from Private Sources.* Princeton, NJ: Peterson's, 1998.

Ragins, Marianne. *Winning Scholarships for College, Third Edition: An Insider's Guide.* New York: Henry Holt & Co., 2004.

Schlacter, Gail, and R. David Weber. *Scholarships 2008.* New York: Kaplan, 1999.

Schwartz, John. *College Scholarships and Financial Aid.* 6th edition. New York: Arco, 1995.

U.S. Department of Education. *Looking for Student Aid.* Washington, D.C.: U.S. Department of Education, [annual]. To get a printed copy of this overview of sources of information about financial aid, call 800-4-FED-AID.

————. *The Student Guide.* Washington, D.C.: U.S. Department of Education, [annual]. To get a printed copy of this handbook about federal aid programs, call 800-4-FED-AID.

Other Related Financial Aid Books

Annual Register of Grant Support. Chicago: Marquis, [annual].

A's and B's of Academic Scholarships. Alexandria, VA: Octameron, [annual].

Chronicle Student Aid Annual. Moravia, NY: Chronicle Guidance, [annual].

College Blue Book. Scholarships, Fellowships, Grants and Loans. New York: Macmillan, [annual].

College Financial Aid Annual. New York: Prentice-Hall, [annual].

Directory of Financial Aids for Minorities. San Carlos, CA: Reference Service Press, [biennial].

Directory of Financial Aids for Women. San Carlos, CA: Reference Service Press, [biennial].

Leider, Robert, and Ann Leider. *Don't Miss Out: The Ambitious Student's Guide to Financial Aid.* Alexandria, VA: Octameron, [annual].

Financial Aids for Higher Education. Dubuque: Wm. C. Brown, [biennial].

Financial Aid for the Disabled and their Families. San Carlos, CA.: Reference Service Press, [biennial].

Peterson's Guides. *Paying Less for College.* Princeton, NJ: Peterson's, [annual].

INSIDE TRACK

Kenneth D. Riddle Jr.
Deputy Fire Chief
Las Vegas Fire & Rescue

While in high school I became interested in the medical profession as result of a class in which students were allowed to work in the local hospital. I liked it so much that I became a Red Cross volunteer and spent many hours working in various areas of the hospital, including the emergency room and the laboratory. In my senior year of high school, I applied for a job at the hospital and was hired as an Orderly (now called a Nursing Assistant). While working in the ER I decided to become an Emergency Medical Technician (EMT). I attended EMT training and was hired at age 18 by Mercy Ambulance in Las Vegas, and worked there from 1974 to 1978. In 1978, I started working with the Las Vegas Fire Department as a firefighter-paramedic. Since being hired I have also held the positions of EMS Training Officer (a Captain's rank), EMS Battalion Chief, Assistant Fire Chief, and Deputy Fire Chief.

I really liked being a firefighter-paramedic because you could actually help someone who needed assistance, especially when it involved life-saving assistance. It always made me feel good when I was able to save someone's life. Of course, I would get upset at not being able to save everyone. The long hours also became something to dislike as I got older.

As a Deputy Fire Chief, I am responsible for the medical aspects of the fire department, including the EMS program, health and wellness, and safety. I am also in charge of a new program the department is developing for responding to medical incidents resulting from the use of weapons of mass destruction. A typical shift for me begins at 8:00 A.M. Usually, I return phone calls in the morning, check my schedule for the day, and provide assistance to my staff. My current staff consists of a doctor, nurse, EMS Battalion Chief, a Fire Training Officer, and a Stress Management Coordinator. I get my job satisfaction in this position by helping my staff to be successful. I spend most of my time maintaining and enhancing current programs and planning new programs, of which there are many for the progressive fire department.

My advice to anyone interested in EMS or the fire service is to start young. Attend courses and programs and join organizations that are related to the field. You must have an advanced education to be competitive—the education often gives you an advantage during the application process, and it also improves your abilities and performance. The biggest change to the EMS and the fire service is the use of technology and the expansion of services. The technology available today makes the job of firefighting safer and the EMS tasks more reliable. Unfortunately this technology is often out of the financial reach of many agencies. Another major change is the role of the fire service today—modern fire service agencies do much more than just fight fires—from medical services and prevention education to social services and community programs, the fire service has changed a lot, and it will keep on changing and growing into the future.

CHAPTER **five**

SUCCEEDING ON THE JOB

YOU'RE READY to begin your career as a firefighter. This chapter will guide you from your first days as a probie to years down the road, when you're looking at promotions. The qualities of successful firefighters are explained, along with the steps you need to follow in order to move up in the ranks. Advancement opportunities and other fire-related career options are clearly explained.

CAREER FIREFIGHTERS, those who stay in the firefighting field until retirement, follow many of the same basic steps and have many of the same strengths. Learning the secrets of their success can be the first step in including yourself in their ranks. To start, you'll need to do well in your job as a probationary firefighter. It is only after you make it through the probationary period that you are fully admitted and sworn in as an official firefighter in good standing. Then you may become eligible for a wealth of advancement options, from attaining Firefighter II certification to becoming a lieutenant, captain, or fire chief. Several other fire-related career paths are open to you as well, from fire code enforcement officer to arson investigator and more. But it all begins with the probationary period.

SUCCEEDING AS A PROBATIONARY FIREFIGHTER

After you are hired by a fire department, you'll most likely begin a fire training course. In large urban fire departments, new recruits are normally trained for several weeks at the department's own training center. Smaller fire departments may send you to a state or county fire academy. Either way, this training is often considered boot camp for new firefighters. The physical demands are rigorous and may include a variety of tasks, such as using axes, saws, chemical extinguishers, ladders, and other equipment during simulated emergencies. Classroom work is normally required as well.

Training of new firefighters differs from state to state because some require job applicants to obtain Firefighter I certification before they can be hired, while others won't allow you to be certified as a firefighter until after you are hired. Regardless of the amount and intensity of the training you receive as a newly hired firefighter, you will learn the standard operating procedures (SOP) for your department and gain skills that should help to prepare you for success in your new career.

Fitting into the Fire House Culture

Newly hired firefighters undergo a period of probation, ranging from 6 to 18 months. Most probies get through this period and are sworn in as official firefighters, but it is also possible that either the firefighter or the hiring department may decide that he or she isn't cut out to be a firefighter. Therefore it is crucial that you do your best, apply yourself, foster a teamwork attitude, and follow orders during your probationary period.

In many fire departments, the practice of breaking in the probies is similar to the way fraternity members deal with new pledges. Essentially harmless taunting and practical joking are commonplace, and although it may be difficult, the best way to deal with it is to quickly develop a strong sense of humor. (We're not speaking here about dangerous hazing behavior, which is very rare and can be illegal.) You don't want to make enemies or get a reputation as someone who can't take a joke. Because teamwork is so important to firefighters, much of the teasing and the practical jokes are a way to feel out new firefighters to see how they'll take it and whether they'll be a good sport about it.

Learning from Mentors

Finding and learning from a mentor can be an essential element in your success. A mentor is someone you see as successful and with whom you create an informal teacher-student relationship. Enter into the relationship intending to observe your mentor carefully, and ask a lot of questions. The following is a list of things you may learn from a mentor:

- ▶ public interaction skills
- ▶ how to study for promotional exams
- ▶ what to expect in the fire house culture
- ▶ how to communicate with the chain of command in your department
- ▶ in-depth knowledge about equipment and technology used by your department
- ▶ helpful tips for repair and maintenance of equipment and supplies
- ▶ what are the best firefighter magazines and other resource materials
- ▶ what conferences, classes, or training programs you should attend

You'll probably need to actively search for a mentor in your fire house, unless someone decides to take you under his or her wing and show you the ropes. A mentor can be anyone from a battalion chief to one of your peers. There is no formula for who makes a good mentor; it is not based on title, level of seniority, or years in the department. Instead, the qualities of a good mentor are based on a combination of willingness to be a mentor, level of expertise in a certain area, teaching ability, and attitude.

When looking for a mentor, keep in mind the following questions:

- ▶ When asked a question, does the potential mentor take the time to help you find a resolution rather than point you toward someone else who can help you?
- ▶ Does the potential mentor tackle problems in a reasonable manner until they are resolved?
- ▶ What is it that people admire about the potential mentor? Do the admirable qualities coincide with your values and goals?
- ▶ Is he or she strong in areas in which you are weak?

Once you've entered into a relationship with a mentor, you should learn as much as you can from him or her. Keep in mind that, after a while, career growth may open up different possibilities in new areas of specialization. If that happens, you'll probably want to find additional mentors who can show you the ropes in the new environment. However, any former mentors you can keep as friends will not only help you with your career, but can also enrich your life. An experienced firefighter from San Jose, California, recollects the following about his first mentor:

> I'll never forget my first mentor in the fire department. I felt so green when I started, and I was afraid of messing up all the time. Then I sought out a senior firefighter who had been with the department for 18 years and began asking him simple questions about how things were run. He was a little gruff at first, but I think he was flattered that I asked him stuff. Pretty soon, he started telling me stories about how things worked around the place, and I got lots of tips and inside information about what the chief was like and how I should respond to the different firefighters and the captain on our shift. I'm still friends with him to this day, even though he retired a long time ago.

INTERACTING WITH SUPERVISORS

The most important action you can take to help you interact successfully with a supervisor, whether he or she is a captain or a battalion chief, an incident commander at the site of an emergency or a fire chief, is to follow that person's orders quickly and carefully. Because firefighting is a dangerous activity, following the orders of superior officers is of utmost importance. Some new firefighters think they can do things better than the way they are currently being done. When you begin your firefighting career, be careful not to make brash claims about the superiority of your ideas. Instead, lie low for a while, finding out the motivations behind the orders and seeing the results of those orders in action.

When you're not in the midst of an emergency, there are different ways to interact with your supervisors. Some fire stations have an informal atmosphere in which everyone interacts, regardless of rank. Other fire houses are more formal, and you need to be on your guard when addressing company officers. You'll get a feel for the atmosphere in your fire house after a few weeks on the job. Until you know for sure, play it safe by assuming a more formal manner when addressing your supervisors.

INTERACTING WITH THE PUBLIC

Public interaction is an important part of the firefighter's job. Whether it's in an emergency situation or during a public fire prevention talk, firefighters are highly respected. You don't want to do anything that might endanger that sense of respect. This is especially important during times of government downsizing and budget-cutting, when public support is crucial to the success of both municipal and volunteer fire departments.

One way in which fire departments can foster public support is through their collective, positive actions on emergency calls. Firefighters who offer help and comfort to victims in emergency situations, in addition to providing professional emergency assistance, generate good will from the citizens being helped as well as from people in the vicinity who witness such help. For example, firefighters who take the time to explain what is happening after a fire occurs or who retrieve someone's prized wedding album from wreckage can go a long way toward building respect and support in the community.

You'll find that many fire departments focus increasingly on good public relations during an emergency in order to build taxpayer support for municipal departments and healthier donations for volunteer departments. Being a conscientious worker and developing a high standard of work performance, along with displaying a caring attitude during emergencies, can be integral parts of your success as a firefighter.

DEVELOPING THE QUALITIES THAT COUNT

As you progress through your firefighting career, knowing the qualities that are rewarded will give you an edge. There are several things you can do to increase your educational background, technical skills, and effectiveness as a firefighter, as noted in Chapter 3. The personal qualities that are rewarded in fire departments follow the rules of common sense. Some of these qualifications are

- ▶ honesty in your dealings with other firefighters, supervisors, and the public
- ▶ mental alertness, which, when you're on duty, can mean the difference between life and death
- ▶ respect for the chain of command: the incident commander at an emergency has the most information to insure the giving of proper orders
- ▶ compliance with safety precautions, in order to save lives and reduce injuries
- ▶ willingness to learn from mistakes: noting what went wrong during an emergency call, and analyzing why it did, can help to ensure that it doesn't happen again
- ▶ good listening skills: if important safety points and orders need to be repeated, time is wasted, which may cost lives

KNOWING WHEN TO BE READY

According to the U.S. Fire Administration, fire calls peak between 5 and 7 P.M. from the surge in cooking-related fires during the dinner period. Broken down by season, residential fires are most frequent during the winter, when heating is a dominant cause. For example, the residential fire rate for January is almost twice that of summer months, and the fire death rate for January is triple that of summer months.

MAINTAINING PERSONAL HEALTH AND FITNESS

Firefighters need to maintain good health and physical fitness in order to perform their tasks well. Some fire departments provide on-site facilities, such as weight training equipment or other fitness machines, to help firefighters stay in shape. If your department doesn't, consider joining a fitness center nearby or planning regular workouts with other firefighters. You may need to take and pass physical ability tests on a regular basis or in order to achieve a promotion in some fire departments, so you'll want to be ready.

Eating balanced meals and getting enough sleep are constant challenges to the modern firefighter. If you are on a work schedule in which you eat meals together at the fire house, suggest healthful alternatives to the regular diet. Your energy and stamina come from the food you eat, so it should be optimal fuel for your body. The right amount of sleep also affects energy and stamina, so you'll need to make a good effort to get the sleep hours you need.

JUST THE FACTS

In 1970, California firefighters established the Firefighter's Olympic Games as a way to promote physical fitness and have a friendly competition that could double as a casual convention of colleagues. The Firefighter's Olympics now boasts both summer and winter games, including such varied events as bowling, bass fishing, rodeo, and water skiing. The Firefighter's Olympics are held in California.

ADVANCEMENT OPPORTUNITIES

Some firefighters are very satisfied with their job and make fighting fires their lifelong career. Others may join up with a municipal fire department as a firefighter and then move into a position of higher rank, such as lieutenant or captain. The advancement route firefighters can pursue varies, depending on the size and location of their fire department, but usually follows this path: level-two firefighter, apparatus operator (or engineer), lieutenant or captain, battalion chief, assistant chief, deputy chief, and, finally, fire chief. Of course, not everyone advances to become a fire chief, but many firefighters do advance to the level of apparatus operator, lieutenant, or captain.

Advancement opportunities for firefighters often depend on several factors:

▶ seniority
▶ scores on promotional exams
▶ recommendations from supervisors
▶ job performance
▶ the number of openings in higher positions

▶ growth of the department
▶ education level

You may have all the qualifications, motivation, and skills needed for a promotion in your department, yet find that there are no openings at the next level. When that happens, you can either wait for an opening to occur or you can apply for a job in another fire department that has more advancement opportunities. According to a firefighter in Florida, it may be worth it to stay in your department and wait for an opening, if you really enjoy your work and the people you work with. He says:

> I joined my department at a time when there were already several people who had just been promoted, so I had to wait nine years before I was able to land a promotion to apparatus operator. Then it was another eight years before I made it to lieutenant. Now I see guys getting promoted to those positions within only three or four years of being hired, because so many people are retiring or moving on now. It's really a cyclical thing, so if early promotion is extremely important to you, try to find out how many people have been promoted recently in your fire department. If it doesn't look good, you may want to try and transfer to another department right away, before you get too settled in. However, if you don't mind the wait, there's great security in staying where you are and not moving around.

You may want to consider applying to another fire department for a number of reasons. Realize that by getting a job in another fire department, you can, in essence, give yourself a promotion. Even if it's a lateral move, you may enjoy one or more of these benefits from a move:

▶ better pay
▶ preferable health benefits and work schedule
▶ superior training programs
▶ improved firefighting equipment
▶ better camaraderie with coworkers and supervisors
▶ more room for advancement

Of course, if you land your first job in a great fire department that offers many benefits and advancement opportunities, then you're all set. You can focus on learning all you can and preparing yourself for future promotional opportunities or career challenges in related areas. Should you decide to seek advancement in the firefighting field, the promotion process is explained in the next section.

How to Prepare for a Promotion

Many experienced firefighters study regularly to improve their job performance and prepare for promotion examinations. In general, firefighters today need more training to operate increasingly sophisticated equipment and to deal safely with the greater hazards associated with fighting fires in larger, more elaborate structures. To progress to higher-level positions, firefighters need to acquire expertise in the most advanced fire-fighting equipment and techniques, building construction, emergency medical procedures, writing, public speaking, management, budgeting procedures, and labor relations.

IN THE NEWS

Considered one of the best advancements in firefighting equipment in recent years, the thermal imaging camera allows firefighters to detect people when they cannot see them. The cameras distinguish items of various temperatures within a room, leading rescuers to human victims in rooms filled with thick smoke. They can also show firefighters where the fire's hot spots are, where the most intense effort is needed—without the firefighters having to break through a structure. The downside? Thermal imaging cameras cost up to $25,000 each.

Fire departments frequently conduct training programs, several colleges and schools offer fire science training programs, and the National Fire Academy sponsors relevant training programs on various topics, including executive development, anti-arson techniques, and public fire safety and education. Some states also provide extensive firefighting training programs at all levels. For instance, in Maryland, the Maryland Fire Service Personnel

Qualifications Board offers training and certification for several areas of specialization, including but not limited to

Driver/Operator	Fire Instructor I, II, III, IV
Airport Firefighter	Hazmat Responder
Fire Officer I, II, III, IV	Hazmat Technician
Fire Inspector I, II, III	Hazmat Incident Commander
Fire Investigator	EMS Hazmat I, II
Public Fire Educator I, II, III	Advanced Exterior Fire Brigade

Taking Promotional Exams

Once you've decided to try for a particular promotion, you'll need to set up a plan for obtaining that goal. These five things can help your chances of scoring high on a promotional exam:

1. Get an idea of what will be on the promotional exam. You can ask people who have already taken the exam what areas were emphasized and what books they recommend that you study in order to prepare for the exam. You may be able to get old tests that have been published for students to review. You may even be fortunate enough to get a suggested reading list along with the exam materials, although this is rare.
2. Set priorities on what material to study. You can't possibly learn every detail about the job, so focus on the most important aspects. This will help prevent your getting bogged down in details that are not going to be tested on the promotional exam.
3. Study test preparation books to find out or brush up on the skills needed to succeed on written exams. For example, look up information on how to handle test anxiety, how to score as high as possible on multiple-choice questions, and how to take tests within specific time limits. See Appendix C for resources.
4. Make a study schedule several months before the exam, and stick to it. Allow sufficient time each day for studying a section of material, and don't forget to preview and review the material you study each day. A

good study method is to create flash cards and test yourself on key concepts and questions you think may appear on the test.

5. Find out if your fire department uses assessment centers to test practical, hands-on aspects of the job you are applying for. If so, talk to people who have gone through the assessment center to get their advice on how you can prepare for this segment of the process. You should also find out if you are allowed to tour the assessment facility to get an idea of what equipment will be used to test you.

JOB DESCRIPTIONS FOR ADVANCED POSITIONS

To get a better idea of where your future firefighting career could lead you, read the following job descriptions of key advancement opportunities in the field.

The following average salaries are for full-time, sworn-in personnel and were gathered in 2006 from a nationwide survey.

Position	Minimum Annual Base Salary	Maximum Annual Base Salary
Fire chief	$73,435	$95,271
Deputy chief	$66,420	$84,284
Assistant fire chief	$61,887	$78,914
Battalion chief	$62,199	$78,611
Fire captain	$51,808	$62,785
Fire lieutenant	$47,469	$56,511
Fire prevention code inspector	$45,951	$58,349
Engineer	$43,232	$56,045

Apparatus Operator

Apparatus operators drive the fire truck to emergency calls. They are also referred to as engineers or chauffeurs in some departments. Their skill level goes well beyond merely driving the fire truck, however. They also maintain, inspect, and perform minor repairs on emergency vehicles to ensure a high level of performance. They are responsible for operating pumps, aerial ladders, and/or other equipment during fire suppression calls. Various national certifications for this position are available, including the following:

- ▶ Driver/Operator—Pumper
- ▶ Driver/Operator—Aerial
- ▶ Driver/Operator—Tiller
- ▶ Driver/Operator—ARF
- ▶ Driver/Operator—Wildland

Apparatus operators are paid a higher salary than firefighters because of the specialized knowledge they need and the greater amount of responsibility they have.

Lieutenant or Captain

Lieutenants and captains are referred to as company officers. They supervise firefighters and issue orders to their crew at the scene of emergencies. The size of each lieutenant or captain's crew varies considerably, depending on the size and location of the fire department. However, they all need to be well versed in how to handle emergency situations and how to manage personnel, as these two activities make up a large portion of their job. They may also be responsible for training new firefighters in fire house procedures, inspecting fire house equipment, and making requests for additional or newer equipment. Lieutenants and captains are normally paid considerably more than firefighters (at least 20 to 25%), because of the higher level of responsibility and added management duties their job requires.

Battalion Chief

Battalion chiefs hold the next highest rank after lieutenants and captains. They are responsible for a group of lieutenants and captains as well as the firefighters who work under them. Battalion chiefs coordinate and supervise the fire companies under their command during emergency calls and keep communication lines open between lieutenants or captains and superior officers. They are often responsible for recommending personnel for awards; inspecting records, equipment, and personnel in their jurisdiction; issuing purchase orders; and preparing reports of accidents or other noteworthy incidents. They may also assist the fire chief in creating and maintaining departmental budgets and other administrative tasks as needed. Battalion chiefs earn approximately 10 to 15% more than lieutenants or captains because of the higher level of responsibility involved in their job.

Deputy Fire Chief or Assistant Fire Chief

Deputy or assistant fire chiefs perform many of the same functions as the fire chief. They are found mostly in large urban fire departments, because fire chiefs need help in departments that employ large numbers of firefighters and cover densely populated areas. Some deputy fire chiefs are responsible for a particular sector of the department, such as operations or training, or they may cover a particular district. See the following description under the fire chief heading for the types of duties that many deputy and assistant chiefs perform.

Fire Chief

The fire chief is on the top rung of the career ladder for firefighters. Fire chiefs are responsible for entire fire departments, including all firefighters, lieutenants, captains, battalion chiefs, and any deputy or assistant fire chiefs. Therefore their duties are numerous and varied. The specific job duties of fire chiefs depend on the size and type of fire department they are managing. In general, fire chiefs are normally responsible for managing the resources of the department, preparing the departmental budget, commanding multiple-alarm fires, administering laws and regulations in their department, and acting as liaison for the fire department with public officials. Salaries for fire chiefs vary greatly. A fire chief in charge of several thousand firefighters is going to command a much higher salary than one who manages a staff of fewer than a hundred. Many fire chiefs earn a significant salary because of their many years of experience and high level of education. Some earn close to or even more than $100,000 annually. Of course, fire chiefs in small rural areas earn considerably less.

Sample Job Postings for Advanced Positions

These postings can give you an idea of the requirements and salaries available with advancement opportunities. Of course, salaries vary considerably depending on location and size of the fire department, but these descriptions can give you a good idea of what to expect.

Position	Firefighter/Paramedic
Location	Florida
Requirements	State of Florida firefighter certification from the Bureau of Fire Standards and Training; current state of Florida paramedic certification (or proof of enrollment as a third-semester paramedic student)
Salary	$21,730–44,340 (includes paramedic assignment pay)
Position	Safety Division Manager/Fire Marshal
Location	Oregon
Description	Responsible for the fire department's Safety Division, which includes all operations related to the prevention of fire and life safety issues for the public and any related safety issues for the fire department employees; coordinates and organizes logistical aspects of the department's needs; and does related work as required
Requirements	Associate degree in emergency services field (bachelor's degree preferred); 10 years' experience in fire service, with background in fire prevention, fire codes and ordinances, training, budgeting, field supervision, and planning; state-certified Fire Officer I; state-certified EMT-B; possession of valid state driver's license; must pass physical exam, including drug testing, and be a nonsmoker
Salary	$52,068–68,020

Position	Fire Protection Engineer
Location	California
Description	Participates directly in the review of building and development plans for compliance with state and local fire codes and other permit requirements, conducts highly technical fire prevention activities, and provides highly technical staff assistance
Requirements	Equivalent of a bachelor's degree, with major in fire protection engineering or a closely related field; sufficient fire prevention and plan review experience to demonstrate knowledge of principles of modern fire prevention, fire protection engineering, and fire suppression activities, knowledge of fire codes and applicable state laws; and ability to make studies and prepare reports, enforce codes, ordinances, and regulations, and represent the fire department to contractors, engineers, architects, and developers
Salary	$69,588–87,930
Position	Fire Chief
Location	Arizona
Description	Plans, directs, and controls departmental activities, including recruitment of personnel, purchase of equipment, and assignment of personnel and equipment; coordinates activities with other town departments and outside agencies to ensure effective working relationships and mutual aid agreements; develops appropriate contract documents for administrative and operational needs and routinely upgrades them; evaluates needs and makes recommendations for location and construction of fire stations and purchase of apparatus and equipment; conducts, supervises, and reviews the town's fire department in-service training program; resolves citizen complaints and problems concerning activities of the department; and coordinates with code enforcement in the development, revision, and enforcement of town fire and building codes.
Requirements	Bachelor's degree in fire science, public administration, or business administration; a minimum of eight years of increasingly responsible command and supervisory experience in a professional municipal fire department; five years' experience as chief, deputy chief, or assistant chief preferred
Salary	$73,505–101,518

CAREER OPTIONS

Fire service is a broad and still-expanding field that offers numerous career choices. In general, firefighter training offers a good basic background for other fire service careers. Certain career paths involve returning to college or even graduate school for more in-depth study of subjects such as biology and chemistry only touched upon by firefighting academies. There are also civilian career paths in fire service that have specific higher education or certification requirements but don't necessarily require firefighter training.

Here are descriptions of several fire-related careers. Note that some options require several years of firefighting experience, while others require highly specialized training.

Fire Prevention Specialists

Fire prevention specialists work with a variety of people to teach fire prevention techniques. Many lecture at schools, nonprofit groups, civic organizations, and senior living residences. They also work with home and business owners to ensure that vegetation around buildings and homes are cut down and that open spaces between structures are not overgrown with long, dry grass—the fuel of those large wildfires that plague many parts of the country every year.

The priorities for prevention programs are tailored to different locations and purposes. Fire prevention specialists teach people the leading causes of fires—cooking, heating, and arson—and the leading causes of fire deaths—careless smoking, heating, and arson. These causes are relatively similar across the nation.

Typical Minimum Requirements

The minimum requirements for the position of fire prevention specialist vary from department to department. Some fire departments require that these positions be filled with experienced firefighters through a promotion and application process, which could take several years to complete. Other fire departments open the position of fire prevention specialist to graduates of fire science degree programs who haven't ever served as firefighters. Fire prevention specialists normally have some formal education, public speaking skills, and teaching experience in their background.

Fire Code Enforcement Officers

Fire code enforcement officers oversee the more technical aspects of fire prevention and are similar to fire inspectors. They often review building plans to designate and ensure compliance with fire safety codes and protection systems. They also assess the number and placement of fire exits and establish the maximum number of occupants allowed in a building. Some states refer to their fire inspectors as fire code enforcement officers, while others differentiate between the two.

Typical Minimum Requirements

Minimum requirements for becoming a fire code enforcement officer vary among departments and states. However, applicants normally need to have either sufficient training from a recognized training program or several years of experience in the field before attaining the level of fire code enforcement officer.

Fire Marshals

The duties of fire marshals vary greatly depending on what state they work in. In some states, the fire marshal may be appointed by one of the following:

▶ a state's attorney general
▶ a state fire board
▶ a fire prevention commission
▶ some other governing body

Many fire marshals serve as investigators, determining the origin of a fire, whether fire laws have been violated, and whether a fire is the result of criminal negligence or arson. In some states, fire marshals are given powers of subpoena and arrest to investigate the cause of a fire. Marshals may test sites for flammable gases or liquids and are trained to evaluate burn patterns to show where a fire started and how it burned. They report their findings to the district attorney if criminal charges should be filed and are often familiar with laws and court procedures. Many fire marshals also inspect commercial buildings to enforce state fire prevention codes as well as performing other administrative duties.

Typical Minimum Requirements

The minimum requirements for becoming a fire marshal vary greatly nationwide. In most states, they are required to have extensive experience in fire service and public safety or related areas. Consult the sample job postings beginning on page 158 for the requirements specified by a fire department in Oregon.

Arson Investigators

Arson investigators may work in conjunction with the fire marshal's office or in a fire department's fire prevention division. They investigate the causes of fires and explosions to find out whether criminal activity was involved. Their investigative responsibilities are often similar to those performed by fire marshals in some states. Arson investigators use their analytical skills and knowledge of fire science to make judgments and create reports about the fires they investigate. Many arson investigators interview involved parties to determine the probable cause of a fire. They sometimes testify as expert witnesses in court cases.

Typical Minimum Requirements

Arson investigators are often promoted from a position within a fire department or fire prevention division. Therefore they often possess firefighting skills or knowledge of fire science practices and procedures. Some states may hire investigators from fire-related fields other than firefighting. Specialized knowledge in how fires are started and how they spread is needed. Organization and analytical skills are also helpful. Most arson investigators have some level of college training.

Hazardous Materials Specialists

Firefighters who deal with dangerous situations involving hazardous materials, called *hazmat* in the field, require specialized training and equipment. Therefore fire departments usually employ specially trained personnel who are called in to clean up spills or leaks such as deadly waste dumped from refineries and chemical or nuclear plants.

This growing field is heavily regulated by state and national agencies and requires proper certification, which can be achieved through extension programs at many public colleges. In addition to college training courses, many fire departments take it upon themselves to train their hazmat personnel in their own safety and emergency-response procedures.

Typical Minimum Requirements

Certification in hazardous materials often involves a combination of hands-on and classroom learning from a fire academy, community college, or correspondence course. Some programs offer different levels of certification in hazardous materials, such as

- ▶ Hazmat Responder—Awareness
- ▶ Hazmat Responder—Operational
- ▶ Hazmat—Technician
- ▶ Hazmat Incident Commander
- ▶ Hazmat Off-Site Specialist, Employees

Crash, Fire, and Rescue Firefighters

Specialized knowledge is needed to become an airport firefighter who deals with airplane crashes and fires. These firefighters conduct rescue efforts of plane crews and passengers in the event of an emergency. They may respond to potential air crash emergencies by spraying foam on the runway to minimize the chances of an explosion, or to actual air crash emergencies by spraying chemical solutions or water fog onto the aircraft. They offer emergency medical procedures to victims and may be involved in deactivating aircraft electrical power to prevent explosions. Crash, fire, and rescue firefighters may be employed by commercial, military, or general airports.

Typical Minimum Requirements

Firefighters who want to specialize in the crash, fire, and rescue area need to obtain training and experience to prepare them for the intricacies of the job. Training programs are offered throughout the nation to help firefighters learn the specialized information and skills needed to respond to air crash, fire, and rescue needs at airports. A firefighter can become certified as an airport firefighter by meeting the standards set by the National Board on Fire Service Professional Qualifications, a division of the National Fire Protection Association (NFPA).

Fire Insurance Company Representatives

Several hiring opportunities are available in fire insurance companies for firefighters, or others interested in the firefighting field. For example, fire insurance claim examiners are needed to analyze claims, decide which are valid, and in some cases settle claims after reviewing available data and interviewing both claimants and agents.

Claims adjusters are also needed in the fire insurance area. They are responsible for negotiating settlements after inspecting property damage and other incidents related to a fire. Adjusters usually have to prepare comprehensive reports about each case they get.

A third insurance company representative is the fire science specialist, who may help the insurance company set rates for fire-related coverage. He or she may also examine fire prevention methods, such as sprinkler systems, at various places of business and offer suggestions for improving hazardous conditions.

Typical Minimum Requirements

There are no hard-and-fast rules about who can become a fire insurance company representative. Because of the variety of employers, people with a variety of backgrounds and requirements are needed. In general, you'll need some training or background in fire science and fire investigation work.

Some companies may offer on-the-job-training to fill in the gaps in your background. Many companies look favorably on applicants who have completed an associate degree in fire science or a related area.

Fire Services Instructors

Firefighters who are interested in education may wish to become instructors within their fire departments or at a nearby community college or other fire training school. Instructors who work in fire departments are often called training officers. They provide training to all levels of firefighters, from new recruits to senior firefighters who need help with new materials. Rank depends on the size and location of the fire department, but instructors are often at the level of captain or higher.

In addition to teaching in a classroom or lab facility, instructors may also organize training programs for specific groups of people or specific tasks. For example, they may need to organize a training program for newly hired recruits or for firefighters who want to apply for the position of apparatus operator or lieutenant. Instructors at colleges or fire academies perform similar teaching functions and may be involved in organizing or updating training programs.

Typical Minimum Requirements

Since firefighter instructors need a wealth of knowledge in order to teach others, they must have a solid foundation in the subject matter they are teaching. Therefore they would benefit from several years of working as a firefighter before becoming an instructor. For instructors in specialized fields, such as hazardous materials or crash and rescue operations, additional education and field experience are needed. Instructors can obtain certification according to standards set by the National Fire Protection Association (NFPA).

Wildland Smoke Jumper Supervisors

Smoke jumper supervisors coordinate airborne firefighting crews during wildland fires. They examine the location, size, and condition of a wildfire, so they know how many smoke jumpers to employ in each area of the fire.

They oversee the process of dropping equipment from aircraft to the smoke jumpers on the ground as well as retrieving smoke jumpers from the field after a fire is placed under control. Smoke jumper supervisors may be involved in combating actual fires along with their subordinates. They maintain open lines of communication between the smoke jumpers in the field and the crews back at the base of operations. They also train new smoke jumpers in

▶ parachute jumping
▶ wildland fire suppression
▶ aerial observation of fires
▶ radio communications

Typical Minimum Requirements

Smoke jumper supervisors need extensive experience both as smoke jumpers and as wildland firefighters. It may take several years to land a job as a smoke jumper, because of the extremely intense physical fitness level required and the competitive nature of the job. Therefore a person may need to serve for several years as a seasonal wildland firefighter before becoming a smoke jumper.

Forest Fire Warden or Fire Ranger

Fire wardens and rangers are needed in forests and other wildland areas to take fire prevention measures and to scout for dangerous fire conditions. They perform inspections of campsites, logging areas, and other remote areas to help prevent and to report fires. In the case of a forest fire, they may become crew leaders and issue commands on the fire line and in the base camp. They normally examine and maintain firefighting equipment and supplies to ensure accordance with company and government regulations. They may need to give first aid to accident victims.

Typical Minimum Requirements

Typical minimum requirements for a fire warden or ranger depend on whether you want to work on state, federal, or private lands. Many forest fire wardens and deputies have experience as seasonal wildland firefighters, and they become certified through various agencies.

Succeeding in Every Step of Your Career

Now that you've learned about many of the advancement opportunities available to firefighters, it's time to think seriously about the direction you'd like your career to take. Some people working in fire services prefer to remain firefighters, in on all the action, until retirement. Others work up the ranks toward fire chief or get hired out of the fire house as investigators, insurance experts, or instructors teaching the next generation of firefighters.

We've outlined the steps you need to follow if you think you might seek a promotion. Do some further research into any or all of the advanced positions that interest you. Even in the first days of your career, you can begin to follow a path toward the future.

INSIDE TRACK

Tom Guldner
New York City Fire Department (FDNY)
Lieutenant-Marine Division Training Officer
President, Marine Firefighting Institute

My family has a history with the FDNY and the NYPD. I actually started as a police officer, and after two years I learned that I had passed the firefighter exam and I switched to the FDNY. After ten years of working in the South Bronx, I was promoted to lieutenant, after which I spent ten more years in another of New York City's poorer neighborhoods, Washington Heights in Manhattan. Eight years ago I transferred to the marine division as a lieutenant on the department's only full-time marine fire/rescue boat.

I love my job. At times it has left me emotionally drained and physically weakened, but I wouldn't trade professions with anyone. The only things I'd like to change are the several injuries I've suffered and the fact that I've had to bury too many of my friends.

A typical day for me begins at 9 A.M. I conduct a roll call of everyone working that tour and assign duties and discuss any matters of importance. After paperwork and "committee work," which consists of cleaning the fire house, tools, and boat, we either go out on surveillance inspections of some of the city's piers, wharves, and waterside facilities or we try to board one of the many vessels in New York harbor for shipboard familiarization training. Some special duties include standing by whenever any dignitaries arrive at or depart from the port, as well as covering fireworks and water displays. Of course, we also respond to boat fires, boats in distress, and water rescues. The majority of my time is spent on training, water rescues, and marine firefighting.

The field has really changed since I began—I go way back. When I first joined the FDNY we were still being dispatched by telegraph bell signals. Masks were a novelty, and usually only one member of the company would wear one. We had no medical training and didn't perform any of the more specialized rescue activities. Back then we got the job done, but I'm glad to see some of the new innovations being introduced.

If you want to be a firefighter, the first thing to do is to check with the department you want to join to determine what skills, licenses, and training you must have. The entrance exams all consist of a written test and a physical test. There are many books and study classes that will help you prepare for the written portion, and you will have to be in top shape for the physical portion.

Appendix A

Employment Resources

INDUSTRY-SPECIFIC RECRUITERS

Careers in Fire Service
PO Box 778
Millbrae, CA 94030
800-997-3373
www.usfirejobs.com and www.firerecruit.com

Firehire
PO Box 1822
Elk Grove, CA 95759
800-755-5891
www.firehire.com

Firehire offers job descriptions, benefits, training information, and recruitment services for a fee to potential firefighters looking for a job.

International Fire and Police Recruitment Administration
1127 South Mannheim Road, Suite 203
Westchester, IL 60154
800-343-HIRE
www.ifpra.org

The Perfect Firefighter Candidate
4475 Dupont Court, Suite 3
Ventura, CA 93003
800-326-8401
Fax: 805-658-7128
www.firecareers.com

Public Safety Recruitment
PO Box 587
East Jordan, MI 49727
800-880-9018
www.psrjobs.com

INTERNET JOB SITES

Federal Jobs Digest
www.jobsfed.com/

If you are looking for a wildland firefighting job from the federal government, you might want to check out this website. Select *Live Jobs*, then *Law Enforcement/Fire*, and then *Fire Protection and Prevention* to see a list of federal fire-related job postings.

Fire Career Assistance Biweekly Job Listing Newsletter Subscription Site
www.firecareerassist.com

Firefighter Jobs
home.pacbell.net/putt1234

Fire-Rescue Village Jobs Page
www.firefighterjobs.com

The Fire Station
home.flash.net/˜jturner/jobs.htm

National Directory of Emergency Services
www1.firejobs.com/ndes/

USA Jobs
www.usajobs.opm.gov

This federal government jobs website includes federal wildland firefighting job opportunities. It is a service provided by the Office of Personnel Management (OPM).

Appendix B

Useful Organizations

GOVERNMENT AGENCIES, PROFESSIONAL ASSOCIATIONS, AND UNIONS

Fire and Aviation Management Program
U.S. Forest Service
U.S. Department of Agriculture
1400 Independence Avenue, SW
Washington, D.C. 20050
202-205-8333
www.fs.fed.us/fire

Fire Department Safety Officers
 Association
PO Box 149
Ashland, MA 01721-0149
508-881-3114
www.fdsoa.org

International Association of Arson
 Investigators
2151 Priest Bridge Drive, Suite 25
Crofton, MD 21114
410-451-3473
www.firearson.com

International Association of Black
 Professional Fire Fighters
Executive Director
PO Box 317703
Cincinnati, OH 45231
513-226-6940
www.iabpff.org

International Association of Fire Chiefs
4025 Fair Ridge Drive, Suite 300
Fairfax, VA 22033-2868
703-273-0911
www.ichiefs.org/contact/index.html

International Association of Fire Fighters
1750 New York Avenue NW
Washington, DC 20006
202-737-8484
www.iaff.org

International Association of Wildland Fire

PO Box 261

Hot Springs, SD 57747

605-890-2348

www.ngdc.noaa.gov

International Fire Service Training Association

IFSTA/Fire Service Programs

930 North Willis

Stillwater, OK 74078

800-654-4055

-or-

405-744-5723

www.imis-ext.osufpp.org

International Society of Fire Service Instructors

2425 Highway 49 E

Pleasant View, TN 37148

800-435-0005

www.isfsi.org

The International Society of Fire Service Instructors (ISFSI) offers a monthly magazine.

Los Angeles Fire Recruitment

24-hour job hotline 323-881-2308

www.ci.la.ca.us

The City of Los Angeles Fire Recruitment website discusses the application process and minimum requirements for becoming a firefighter in L.A. You can also call for an application.

National Association of State Fire Marshals

1319 F Street, NW, Suite 301

Washington, DC 20004

202-737-1226

www.firemarshals.org

The National Association of State Fire Marshals (NASFM) is an organization that works to increase public awareness of the dangers of fire. Its website gives hotel and home safety tips, information on sprinklers, sprinkler ordinances, and smoke and heat detectors.

National Association of State Foresters

Washington, DC

202-624-5415

www.stateforesters.org

National Fire Protection Association

1 Batterymarch Park

Quincy, MA 02269

617-770-3000

www.nfpa.org

National Interagency Fire Center

E-mail: nifc_comments@nifc.bim.gov

www.nifc.gov

National Volunteer Fire Council

7852 Walker Drive, Suite 450

Greenbelt, MD 20770

888-275-6832

E-mail: nvfcoffice@nvfc.org

www.nvfc.org

The website for the National Volunteer Fire Council (NVFC), a nonprofit organization, offers news releases and other information related to volunteer firefighting.

Society of Fire Protection Engineers

7315 Wisconsin Avenue, Suite 620E

Bethesda, MD 20814

301-718-2910

www.sfpe.org

Western Fire Chiefs Association

727 Center Street, Suite 300

Salem, OR 97301

541-948-3146

www.wfca.com

United States Fire Administration

16825 South Seton Avenue

Emmitsburg, MD 21727

301-447-1000

www.usfa.dhs.gov

EDUCATIONAL ACCREDITING AGENCIES

National

Accrediting Commission for Career Schools

  and Colleges of Technology

2101 Wilson Boulevard, Suite 302

Arlington, VA 22201

866-510-0746

www.accsct.org

Accrediting Council for Independent

  Colleges and Schools

750 First Street NE, Suite 980

Washington, DC 20002-4241

202-336-6780

www.acics.org

Distance Education and Training Council

1601 18th Street NW

Washington, DC 20009

www.detc.org

Regional

Commission on Colleges of the Southern

  Association of Colleges and Schools

1866 Southern Lane

Decatur, GA 30033

404-679-4500

www.sacscoc.org

The Higher Learning Commission

30 North LaSalle Street, Suite 2400

Chicago, IL 60602-2504

800-621-7440

-or-

312-263-0456

www.ncacihe.org

Middle States Association of Colleges
and Schools
Commission on Institutions of Higher
Education
3624 Market Street
Philadelphia, PA 19104
267-284-5000
E-mail: info@msche.org
www.msache.org

New England Association of Schools and
Colleges
209 Burlington Road, Suite 201
Bedford, MA 01730-1433
781-271-0022
www.neasc.org

Northwest Commission on Colleges and
Universities
8060 165th Avenue NE, Suite 100
Redmond, WA 98052
425-558-4224
www.nwccu.org

Western Association of Schools and
Colleges

Accrediting Commission for Schools
533 Airport Boulevard
Burlingame, CA 94010
650-696-1060

Accrediting Commission for Community
and Junior Colleges
10 Commercial Boulevard, Suite 204
Novato, CA 94949
415-506-0234

www.accjc.org

Accrediting Commission for Senior
Colleges and Universities
985 Atlanta Avenue, Suite 100
Alameda, CA 94501
510-748-9001

www.wascweb.org

Appendix C

Additional Resources

COLLEGE GUIDES

The College Board College Handbook 2008. New York: The College Board, 2008.

Peterson's Two-Year Colleges 2008. Princeton, NJ: Peterson's, 2007.

Vocational & Technical Schools Set 8th Edition (2 vols). Princeton, NJ: Peterson's, 2007.

DISTANCE LEARNING RESOURCES

Criscito, Pat. *Barron's Guide to Distance Learning: Degrees, Certificates, Courses*. Hauppauge, NY: Barron's Educational Series, 1999.

Distance Learning Programs 2004. Princeton, NJ: Peterson's, 2003.

Thorson, Marcie K. *Campus Free College Degrees: Thorson's Guide to Accredited College Degrees through Distance Learning*. Tulsa, OK: Thorson Guides, 2000.

Williams, Marcia L., Kenneth Paprock, and Barbara Covington. *Distance Learning: The Essential Guide*. Thousand Oaks, CA: Sage Publications, 1999.

CAREER-RELATED RESOURCES

Beatty, Richard H. *The Perfect Cover Letter*, paperback edition. New York: John Wiley & Sons, 2003.

Job Interviews That Get You Hiried. New York: LearningExpress, 2006.

Resumes That Get You Hired. New York: LearningExpress, 2006.

Occupational Outlook Handbook, 2008–09 edition. U.S. Bureau of Labor Statistics. Available online at www.bls.gov/ocohome.htm.

FINANCIAL AID AND SCHOLARSHIPS

FastWeb!—Helping Over 7 Million Students Find Scholarships, Colleges and Jobs!

www.fastweb.com

FinAid! The SmartStudent™ Guide to Financial Aid

www.finaid.org

GrantsNet (source for information on science and medical education)

www.grantsnet.org

List of All U.S. Government Programs Benefiting Students

www.fedmoney.org

Student Loan Finance Association

www.slfaloan.com

U.S. Department of Education Federal Student Financial Aid Homepage

www.ed.gov/offices/OSFAP/Students

Yahoo! Financial Aid page

dir.yahoo.com/education/financial_aid

FIREFIGHTING RESOURCES

Books

Carter, Harry R., and Lynne Murnane, eds. *Firefighting Strategy and Tactics.* Fire Protection Publications, 1998.

Delsohn, Steve. *The Fire Inside: Firefighters Talk about Their Lives*. New York: HarperCollins, 1996.

Dunn, Vincent. *Collapse of Burning Buildings: A Guide to Fireground Safety*. Fire Engineering Book Dept, 1988.

Hall, Richard, ed. *Essentials of Fire Fighting*. International Fire Service Training Association, 2007.

Norman, John. *Fire Officer's Handbook of Tactics*. Tulsa, OK: Pennwell Publishing, 2006.

Pyne, Stephen J. *Fire on the Rim: A Firefighter's Season at the Grand Canyon*. Seattle: University of Washington Press, 1995.

Teie, William C. *Firefighter's Handbook on Wildland Firefighting*. Rescue, CA: Deer Valley Press, 2005.

Periodicals

American Fire Journal
9072 East Artesia Boulevard, Suite 7
Bellflower, CA 90706
562-866-1664

Aviation Fire Journal
PO Box 976
Baldwin Place, NY 10505
www.aviationfirejournal.com

EMS Responder
3 Huntington Quadrangle
Melville, NY 11747
www.emsresponder.com

Fire Chief
PO Box 2100
Skokee, IL 60076
866-505-7173
www.firechief.com

Fire Engineering

Pennwell Corporation

21-00 Rte. 208 South

Fair Lawn, NY 07410

www.fireengineering.com

FireHouse

3 Huntington Quadrangle

Melville, NY 11747

631-845-2700

www.firehouse.com

Fire Technology and *National Fire Protection Association Journal*

National Fire Protection Association

1 Batterymarch Park

PO Box 9101

Quincy, MA 02269-9101

617-770-3000

www.nfpa.org

National Fire and Rescue

3000 Highwoods Boulevard, Suite 300

Raleigh, NC 27604-1029

919-872-5040

www.nfrmag.com

Wildland Firefighter

PO Box 11809

Prescott, AZ 86304-1809

520-636-8000

www.wildlandfirefighter.com

Websites

Fire Service Testing Company, Inc.

www.fstc.com

This website offers information about fire and emergency service personnel testing for entrance and promotional exams. Services include written tests, test software, question banks, and assessments. Online practice tests are available for a fee.

National Wildfire Coordinating Group (NWCG) Training Working Team

training.nwcg.gov

NWCG's computerized Multi-Agency Fire Training Schedule is a list of wildland fire and aviation training courses taught throughout the United States. Courses are hosted by federal, state, and local cooperating agencies. The site is your gateway to all wildland fire training. The schedule is compiled and updated daily at the National Interagency Fire Center (NIFC) in Boise, Idaho, and is hosted on the U.S. Department of the Interior's National Park Service (NPS) Fire Home Page (www.nifc.nps.gov/fire)

The Fire and EMS (Emergency Medical Services) Information Network

www.fire-ems.net

Wildland Firefighters Resource Page

www.geocities.com/yosemite/gorge/5561

The United States Fire Administration National Fire Academy Degrees at a Distance program

www.usfa.fema.gov/nfa/tr_ddp.htm

Yahoo! Fire protection site

dir.yahoo.com/health/public_health_and_safety/fire_protection

TEST PREP MATERIALS

LearningExpress. *Firefighter Exam 3rd Edition*. New York: LearningExpress, 2006.
LearningExpress Website
www.learnatest.com

SKILL BUILDERS

Algebra Success 3rd Edition. New York: LearningExpress, 2008.
Geometry Success 2nd Edition. New York: LearningExpress, 2005.

Math Essentials 3rd Edition. New York: LearningExpress, 2006.

Practical Math Success 3rd Edition. New York: LearningExpress, 2005.

Reasoning Skills Success 2nd Edition. New York: LearningExpress, 2005.

Vocabulary & Spelling Success 4th Edition. New York: LearningExpress, 2006.

501 Challenging Logic & Reasoning Problems 2nd Edition. New York: LearningExpress, 2006.

501 Reading Comprehension Questions 3rd Edition. New York: LearningExpress, 2006.

1001 Math Problems 2nd Edition. New York: LearningExpress, 2004.

1001 Vocabulary & Spelling Questions 2nd Edition. New York: LearningExpress, 2003.

Appendix D

Directory of Fire-Related Training Programs

This section provides a listing of schools in each state that offer fire-related training programs. These programs offer a range of training choices—from certificate to associate and bachelor's degrees—and include fire science, fire technology, fire protection engineering, fire administration, and fire protection technology programs. The schools are listed in alphabetical order by city in each state, so you can quickly locate schools that are near you. All programs provide school name, address, and phone number, so you can contact them directly to get more information and application forms.

This listing is intended to help you begin your search for an appropriate school. The schools included in this listing are not endorsed or recommended by LearningExpress. Nor have we included every school that offers fire science programs in every state. We recommend that you use this list as a starting point but that you do further research to see if there are other schools that you might like to consider.

Always contact the schools you are considering to get current information on program requirements and areas of specialization before you apply. And remember that information provided here may change; use the Internet and college guides to find out more about these schools, and to find others that may offer the program(s) you are interested in.

ALABAMA

Jefferson State Community College

2601 Carson Road

Birmingham, AL 35215-3098

205-853-1200

www.jeffersonstate.edu

Lawson State Community College

3060 Wilson Road SW

Birmingham, AL 35221-1798

205-925-2515

www.ls.cc.al.us

Wallace State Community College

801 Main Street NW

PO Box 2000

Hanceville, AL 35077-2000

866-350-WSCC (866-350-9722)

www.wallacestate.edu

Community College of the Air Force

130 West Maxwell Boulevard

Maxwell Air Force Base, AL 36112-6613

334-953-6436

www.au.af.mil/au.ccaf

Northwest-Shoals Community College

800 George Wallace Road

PO Box 2545

Muscle Shoals, AL 35662

256-331-5200

http://nwscc.edu

Northwest-Shoals Community College

2080 College Road

Phil Campbell, AL 35580

256-331-8967

www.nwscc.edu

Chattahoochee Valley Community College

119 Broad Street

Phenix City, AL 36969-7928

334-291-4900

www.cvcc.cc.al.us

Wallace Community College Selma

3000 Earl Goodwin Parkway

Selma, AL 36703

334-876-9227

http://wccs.edu

Alabama Fire College

2501 Phoenix Drive

Tuscaloosa, AL 35404

800-241-2467

-or-

205-391-3744

www.alabamafirecollege.net

Southern Union State Community College

750 Roberts Street

Wadley, AL 36276

256-395-2211

www.suscc.cc.al.us

ALASKA

Community and Technical College

University of Alaska

3211 Providence Drive

Anchorage, AK 99508-8306

907-786-1800

www.uaa.alaska.edu/ctc

University of Alaska
Tanana Valley Campus
510 Second Avenue
Fairbanks, AK 99701
907-474-7400
www.alaska.edu

University of Alaska Anchorage
Matanuska-Susitna College
PO Box 2889
Palmer, AK 99645-2889
907-745-9726
www.uaa.alaska.edu

ARIZONA

Estrella Mountain Community College
3000 North Dysart Road
Avondale, AZ 85340
623-935-8000
www.emc.maricopa.edu

Cochise College
Douglas, AZ 85607-9724
520-515-0500
www.conchise.cc.as.us

Coconino County Community College
3000 North Fourth Street
Flagstaff, AZ 86003
520-527-1222
www.coco.cc.ac.us

Glendale Community College
6000 West Olive Avenue
Glendale, AZ 85302-3090
623-845-3000
www.gc.maricopa.edu

Northland Pioneer College
203 West Hopi Drive
Holbrook, AZ 86025-0610
520-524-1993
www.northland.cc.az.us

Mohave Community College
1971 Jagerson Avenue
Kingman, AZ 86401-1299
520-757-0847
www.mohave.cc.az.us/mcchome.html

Mesa Community College
1833 West Southern Avenue
Mesa, AZ 85202-4866
480-461-7000
www.mc.maricopa.edu

Phoenix College
1202 West Thomas Road
Phoenix, AZ 85013-4234
602-285-7500
www.maricopa.edu

Rio Salado Community College
640 North First Avenue
Phoenix, AZ 85003
480-517-8000
www.rio.maricopa.edu

Yavapai College
1100 East Sheldon Street
Prescott, AZ 86301-3297
520-776-2158
www.yavapai.cc.az.us

Scottsdale Community College
9000 East Chaparral Road
Scottsdale, AZ 85250-2699
480-423-6100
www.sc.maricopa.edu

Cochise College-Sierra Vista Campus
901 North Colombo
Sierra Vista, AZ 85635-2317
520-515-5412
www.cochise.org

Pima County Community College
2202 West Anklam Road
Tucson, AZ 85706
520-206-7000
www.pima.edu

Arizona Western College
9500 South Avenue 8E
Yuma, AZ 85365
520-317-6000
www.awc.cc.az.us

ARKANSAS
SAU Tech Station
100 Carr Road
Camden, AR 71701
870-574-4500
www.sautech.edu

Cossatot Technical College
PO Box 960
DeQueen, AR 71832
870-584-4471
http://cossatot.ctc.tec.ar.us

Garland County Community College
101 College Drive
Hot Springs, AR 71913-9174
501-760-4155
www.gccc.cc.ar.us

Black River Technical College
1416 Highway 304 East
Pocahontas, AR 72455
870-892-4565
www.brtc.tec.ar.us

CALIFORNIA
Cabrillo College
6500 Soquel Drive
Aptos, CA 95003-3194
831-479-6201
www.cabrillo.cc.ca.us

Bakersfield College
1801 Panorama Drive
Bakersfield, CA 93305-1299
661-395-4301
www.bc.cc.ca.us

University of California
Fire Safety Engineering Science
Davis Hall
Berkeley, CA 94720
510-643-8415
www.ucop.edu

Palo Verde College
One College Drive
Blythe, CA 92225
760-922-6168
www.paloverde.edu

Southwestern College
900 Otay Lakes Road
Chula Vista, CA 91910
619-421-6700
www.swc.cc.ca.us

Compton Community College
1111 East Artesia Boulevard
Compton, CA 90221-5393
310-637-2660
www.compton.cc.ca.us

Solano Community College
P.O. Box 246
Fairfield, CA 94585-3197
707-864-7171
www.solano.cc.ca.us

Fresno City College
1101 East University Avenue
Fresno, CA 93741-0002
559-442-4600
www.fcc.cc.ca.us

Glendale Community College
1500 North Verdugo Road
Glendale, CA 91208-2894
818-240-1000
www.glendale.cc.ca.us

Chabot College
25555 Hesperian Blvd.
Hayward, CA 94545-5001
510-723-6700
www.clpccd.cc.ca.us

Imperial Valley College
380 East Aten Road
PO Box 158
Highway 111 and Aten Road
Imperial, CA 92251-0158
760-352-8320
www.imperial.cc.ca.us

Copper Mountain College
PO Box 1398
6126 Rotary Way
Joshua Tree, CA 92252
760-366-3791
www.cmccd.edu

College of Marin
835 College Avenue
Kentfield, CA 94904
415-457-8811
www.marin.cc.ca.us

Antelope Valley College
3041 West Avenue K
Lancaster, CA 93536
666-722-6300
www.avc.edu

Las Positas College
3033 Collier Canyon Road
Livermore, CA 94550-7650
925-373-5800
www.laspositas.cc.ca.us

Long Beach City College
4901 East Carson Street
Long Beach, CA 90808-1780
562-938-4111
www.lbcc.cc.ca.us

California State University
Department of Industrial Studies
5151 University Drive
Los Angeles, CA 90032-8530
323-343-3000
www.calstatela.edu

Yuba College
2088 North Beale Road
Marysville, CA 95901-7699
530-741-6700
www.yuba.cc.ca.us

Merced College
3600 M Street
Merced, CA 95348-2898
209-384-6190
www.merced.cc.ca.us

Modesto Junior College
435 College Avenue
Modesto, CA 95350-5800
209-549-7028
http://gomjc.org

Monterey Peninsula College
980 Fremont Street
Monterey, CA 93940-4799
831-646-4006
www.mpc.edu

East Los Angeles College
1301 Avenida Cesar Chavez
Monterey Park, CA 91754-6099
323-265-8650
www.elac.cc.ca.us

Merritt College
12500 Campus Drive
Oakland, CA 94619-3196
510-436-2598
www.merritt.edu

Butte Community College
3536 Butte Campus Drive
Oroville, CA 95965-8399
530-895-2511
www.cin.butte.cc.ca.us

Oxnard College
4000 South Rose Avenue
Oxnard, CA 93033-6699
805-488-0911
www.oxnard.cc.ca.us

College of the Desert
43500 Monterey Avenue
Palm Desert, CA 92260-9305
760-773-2519
www.desert.cc.ca.us

Pasadena City College
1570 East Colorado Boulevard
Pasadena, CA 91106
626-585-7123
www.paccd.cc.ca.us

Los Medanos College
2700 East Leland Road
Pittsburg, CA 94565-5197
925-429-2181
www.losmedanos.net

Porterville College
100 East College Avenue
Porterville, CA 93257-6058
559-791-2200
www.pc.cc.ca.us

Shasta College
PO Box 496006
Redding, CA 96049-6006
530-225-4769
www.shastacollege.edu

Riverside Community College
4800 Magnolia Avenue
Riverside, CA 92506-1293
909-222-8615
www.rccd.cc.ca.us

Sierra College
5000 Rocklin Road
Rocklin, CA 95677-3397
916-781-0430
www.sierra.cc.ca.us

American River College
4700 College Oak Drive
Sacramento, CA 95841-4286
916-484-8261
www.arc.losrios.cc.ca.us

Cosumnes River College
8401 Center Parkway
Sacramento, CA 95823-5799
916-688-7410
www.crc.losrios.edu

San Diego Miramar College
10440 Black Mountain Road
San Diego, CA 92126-2999
858-536-7800
www.miramarcollege.net

City College of San Francisco
50 Phelan Avenue
San Francisco, CA 94112-1821
415-239-3000
www.ccsf.cc.ca.us

Mount San Jacinto College
21400 Highway 79
San Jacinto, CA 92383-2399
909-487-6752
www.msjc.cc.ca.us

Palomar Community College
1140 West Mission Road
San Marcos, CA 92069-1487
760-744-1150
www.palomar.edu

College of San Mateo
1700 West Hillsdale Boulevard
San Mateo, CA 94402-3784
650-574-6161
www.gocsm.net

Santa Ana College
1530 West Seventeenth Street
Santa Ana, CA 92706-3398
714-564-6000
www.sacollege.org

Mission College
3000 Mission College Boulevard
Santa Clara, CA 95054-1897
408-748-2700
www.mvmccd.cc.ca.us/mc

Allan Hancock College
800 South College Drive
Santa Maria, CA 93454-6399
805-922-6966
www.hancock.cc.ca.us

Santa Monica College
1900 Pico Boulevard
Santa Monica, CA 90405-1644
310-434-4000
www.smc.edu

Santa Rosa Junior College
1501 Mendocino Avenue
Santa Rosa, CA 95401-4395
707-527-4011
www.santarosa.edu

Columbia College
11600 Columbia College Drive
Sonora, CA 95370
209-588-5231
http://gocolumbia.org

Lake Tahoe Community College
One College Drive
South Lake Tahoe, CA 96150-4524
530-541-4660
www.ltcc.cc.ca.us

San Joaquin Delta Community College
5151 Pacific Avenue
Stockton, CA 95207-6370
209-954-5151
www.deltacollege.org

Cogswell Polytechnical College
1175 Bordeaux Drive
Sunnyvale, CA 94089-1299
408-541-0100
www.cogswell.edu

El Camino College
16007 Crenshaw Boulevard
Torrance, CA 90506-0001
310-660-3414
www.elcamino.cc.ca.us

Los Angeles Valley College
5800 Fulton Avenue
Valley Glen, CA 91401-4096
818-947-2600
www.lavc.cc.ca.us

Victor Valley College
18422 Bear Valley Road
Victorville, CA 92395
760-245-4271
www.vvc.edu

College of the Sequoias
915 South Mooney Boulevard
Visalia, CA 93277-2234
559-730-3700
www.cos.edu

Mt. San Antonio College
1100 North Grand Avenue
Walnut, CA 91789-1399
909-594-5611
http://zeus.mtsac.edu

College of the Siskiyous
800 College Avenue
Weed, CA 96094-2899
530-938-5215
www.siskiyous.edu

Rio Hondo College
3600 Workman Mill Road
Whittier, CA 90601-1699
562-692-0921
www.rh.cc.ca.us

Los Angeles Harbor College
1111 South Figueroa Place
Wilmington, CA 90744-2311
310-522-8214
www.lahc.cc.ca.us

Crafton Hills College
11711 Sand Canyon Road
Yucaipa, CA 92399-1799
909-494-2161
www.craftonhills.edu

COLORADO

Community College of Aurora
16000 East Centretech Parkway
Aurora, CO 80011
303-360-4792
www.cca.ccc.oes.edu

Colorado Mountain College
Summit Campus
Breckenridge Center
103 South Harris Street
PO Box 2208
Breckenridge, CO 80424
970-453-6757
www.coloradomtn.edu/campus_sum/home

Pikes Peak Community College
5675 South Academy Blvd.
Colorado Springs, CO 80906-5498
719-540-7650
www.ppcc.cccoes.edu

Colorado Mountain College
Vail/Eagle Valley Campus
139 Broadway
PO Box 249
Eagle, CO 81631
970-328-6304
www.coloradomtn.edu/campus_vev/home

Aims Community College
PO Box 69
Greeley, CO 80632-0069
970-330-8008
www.aims.edu

Red Rocks Community College

13300 West Sixth Avenue

Lakewood, CO 80228-1255

303-988-6160

www.rrcc.edu

Arapahoe Community College

2500 West College Drive

PO Box 9002

Littleton, CO 80160-9002

303-797-5900

www.arapahoe.edu

CONNECTICUT

Capital Community College

950 Main Street

Hartford, CT 06103

860-906-5000

-or-

800-894-6126

http://webster.commnet.edu

Charter Oak State College

55 Paul Manafort Drive

New Britain, CT 06053

860-832-3800

www.cocs.edu

Gateway Community Technical College

60 Sargent Drive

New Haven, CT 06511

203-285-2010

www.online.commnet.edu

Norwalk State Technical College

188 Richards Avenue

Norwalk, CT 06854-1655

203-857-7060

www.ncc.commnet.edu

Three Rivers Community College

547 New London Turnpike

Norwich, CT 06360

860-823-2860

www.trctc.commnet.edu

Naugatuack Valley Community Technical

College

750 Chase Parkway

Waterbury, CT 06708-3000

203-575-8078

www.nvcc.commnet.edu

University of New Haven

Fire Science Department

300 Orange Avenue

West Haven, CT 06516-1916

203-932-7088

www.newhaven.edu

DELAWARE

Delaware Technical & Community College

Stanton Campus

400 Stanton Christiana Road

Newark, DE 19702

302-857-1000

www.dtcc.edu

DISTRICT OF COLUMBIA

University of the District of Columbia

4200 Connecticut Avenue NW

Washington, DC 20008-1175

202-274-5000

www.udc.edu

FLORIDA

Manatee Community College

Bradenton Campus

5840 Twenty-sixth Street West

Bradenton, FL 34207-1849

941-752-5000

www.mcc.cc.fl.us

Brevard Community College

1519 Clear Lake Road

Cocoa, FL 32922-6597

321-632-1111

www.brevard.cc.fl.us

Wm. T. McFatter Tech Center

6500 Nova Drive

Davie, FL 33317

754-321-5700

www.mcfattertech.com

Daytona Beach Community College

Daytona Beach, FL 32120

904-254-4426

www.dbcc.cc.fl.us

Broward Community College

225 East Las Olas Boulevard

Fort Lauderdale, FL 33301-2298

954-761-7464

www.broward.cc.fl.us

Edison Community College

8099 College Parkway SW

Fort Meyers, FL 33906-6210

941-489-9361

www.edison.edu

Indian River Community College

3209 Virginia Avenue

Fort Pierce, FL 34981

561-462-4740

www.ircc.cc.fl.us

Florida Community College at Jacksonville

501 West State Street

Jacksonville, FL 32202-4030

904-646.2300

www.fccj.cc.fl.us

Palm Beach Junior College

4200 Congress Avenue

Lake Worth, FL 33461-4796

561-967-7222

www.pbcc.cc.fl.us

Lake Sumter Community College

Leesburg Campus

9501 US Highway 441

Leesburg, FL 34788-8751

352-787-3747

www.lscc.edu

Chipola Junior College

3094 Indian Circle

Marianna, FL 32446-2053

850-526-2761

www.chipola.cc.fl.us

Miami Dade Community College
300 NE Second Avenue
Miami, FL 33132-2296
305-237-7478
www.mdcc.edu

James Lorenzo Walker Institute of
  Technology
3702 Estey Avenue
Naples, FL 33942-4457
941-434-4815
www.collier.k12.fl.us

Pasco-Hernando Community College
36727 Blanton Road
New Port Richey, FL 33523-7599
352-567-6701
www.pasco-hernandocc.com

Central Florida Community College
PO Box 1388
Ocala, FL 34478-1388
352-237-2111
www.cfcc.cc.fl.us

Florida State Fire College
11655 NW Gainesville Road
Ocala, FL 34482-1486
352-732-1330
www.fsfc.ufl.edu

Valencia Community College
PO Box 3028
Orlando, FL 32802-3028
407-299-5000
www.valenciacc.edu

St. Johns River Community College
5001 St. Johns Avenue
Palatka, FL 32177-3807
904-312-4200
www.sjrcc.cc.fl.us

Gulf Coast Community College
5230 West Highway 98
Panama City, FL 32401-1058
850-769-1551
www.gc.cc.cc.fl.us

Naval Air Technical Training Center
Naval Air Station Pensacola
230 Chevalier Field Avenue
Pensacola, FL 32508-5113
904-452-7212
www.cnet.navy.mil/cnet/nattc

Pensacola Junior College
1000 College Boulevard
Pensacola, FL 32504-8998
850-484-1000
www.pjc.cc.fl.us

St. Augustine Tech Center
2980 Collins Avenue
St. Augustine, FL 32095-9970
904-824-4401
www.fcti.org

Pinellas Technical Education Center
St. Petersburg Campus
901 Thirty-fourth Street South
St. Petersburg, FL 33711
727-893-2500
www.ptecclw.pinellas.k12.fl.us

St. Petersburg Junior College
PO Box 13489
St. Petersburg, FL 33733-3489
727-341-3239
www.spjc.cc.fl.us

Seminole Community College
100 Weldon Road
Sanford, FL 32773
407-328-2025
www.scc.fl.edu

Sarasota County Technical Institute
4748 Beneva Road
Sarasota, FL 34233
941-924-1365
www.careerscape.org

Hillsborough Community College
PO Box 31127
Tampa, FL 33631
813-253-7004
www.hcc.cc.fl.us

Polk Community College
999 Avenue H NE
Winter Haven, FL 33881-4299
863-297-1009
www.polk.cc.fl.us

Ridge Career Center
7700 State Road 544
Winter Haven, FL 33881
863-299-2512
www.pcsb.k12.fl.us

GEORGIA
Dekalb Community College
555 North Indian Creek Road
Clarkston, GA 30021-2396
404-299-4564
www.gpc.peachnet.edu

Macon State College
100 College Station Drive
Macon, GA 31206
478-471-2700
www.maconstate.edu

Savannah Technical Institute
5717 White Bluff Road
Savannah, GA 31499
912-351-6362
www.savannah.tec.ga.us

HAWAII
Honolulu Community College
874 Dillingham Boulevard
Honolulu, HI 96817-4598
808-845-9129
www.hcc.hawaii.edu

IDAHO
Boise State University
College of Technology
1910 University Drive
Boise, ID 83725
208-426-1011
www.idbsu.edu

Eastern Idaho Tech College
1600 South Twenty-fifth East
Idaho Falls, ID 83404-5788
208-524-3000
www.eitc.edu

Lewis-Clark State College
School of Technology
500 Eighth Avenue
Lewiston, ID 83501-2698
208-799-5272
www.lcsc.edu

Idaho State University
Fire Service Technology
PO Box 8054
Pocatello, ID 82309
208-236-2123
www.isu.edu

College of Southern Idaho
315 Falls Avenue
PO Box 1238
Twin Falls, ID 83303-1238
208-733-9554
www.csi.cc.id.us

ILLINOIS
Southwestern Illinois College
2500 Carlyle Avenue
Belleville, IL 62221-5899
618-235-2700
www.southwestern.cc.il.us

Spoon River College
23235 North County 22
Canton, IL 61520
309-647-4645
www.spoonrivercollege.net

Southern Illinois University
Carbondale Campus
Carbondale, IL 62901-6806
618-536-4405
www.siu.edu

Parkland College
2400 West Bradley Avenue
Champaign, IL 61821-1899
217-351-2482
www.parkland.cc.il.us

City Colleges of Chicago
Harold Washington College
30 East Lake Street
Chicago, IL 60601
312-553-6000
www.ccc.edu/hwashington

Prairie State College
202 South Halstead Street
Chicago Heights, IL 60411-8226
708-709-3516
www.prairie.cc.il.us

McHenry County College
8900 US Highway 14
Crystal Lake, IL 60012-2761
815-455-8716
www.mchenry.cc.il.us

Richland Community College
One College Park
Decatur, IL 62521
217-875-7200
www.richland.cc.il.us

Oakton Community College
1600 East Gulf
Des Plaines, IL 60016-1268
847-635-1703
www.oakton.edu

Illinois Central College
One College Drive
East Peoria, IL 61635-0001
309-694-5235
www.icc.cc.il.us

Elgin Community College
1700 Spartan Drive
Elgin, IL 60123-7193
847-888-7385
www.elgin.cc.il.us

College of DuPage
425 Twenty-second St.
Glen Ellyn, IL 60137
630-858-2800
www.cod.edu

Lewis and Clark Community College
5800 Godfrey Road
Godfrey, IL 62035-2466
618-466-3411
www.lc.cc.il.us

College of Lake County
19351 West Washington Street
Grayslake, IL 60030
847-223-6601
www.clc.cc.il.us

Southeastern Illinois College
3575 College Road
Harrisburg, IL 62946
618-252-6376
www.sic.cc.il.us

Joliet Junior College
1215 Houbolt Road
Joliet, IL 60431-8938
815-729-9020
www.jjc.cc.il.us

Kishwaukee College
21193 Malta Road
Malta, IL 60150
815-825-2086
www.kish.cc.il.us

Illinois Valley Community College
815 North Orlando Smith Avenue
Oglesby, IL 61348-9691
815-224-2720
www.ivcc.edu

William Rainey Harper College
1200 West Algonquin Road
Palatine, IL 60067
847-925-6000
www.harpercollege.com

Moraine Valley Community College
10900 South Eighty-eighth Avenue
Palos Hills, IL 60465
708-974-4300
www.moraine.cc.il.us

John Wood Community College
150 South Forty-eighth Street
Quincy, IL 62301
217-224-6500
www.jwcc.edu

Triton College
2000 Fifth Avenue
River Grove, IL 60171
708-456-0300
www.triton.cc.il.us

Rock Valley College
3301 North Mulford Road
Rockford, IL 61114-5699
815-654-4286
www.rvc.cc.il.us

South Suburban College
15800 South State Street
South Holland, IL 60473
708-596-2000
www.ssc.cc.il.us

Lincoln Land Community College
5250 Shepard Road
PO Box 19256
Springfield, IL 62794-9256
800-727-4161
www.llcc.cc.il.us

Waubonsee Community College
Route 47 at Waubonsee Drive
Sugar Grove, IL 60554
630-466-7900
www.wcc.cc.il.us

INDIANA

Ivy Tech State College
Northeast Indiana
3800 North Anthony Boulevard
Fort Wayne, IN 46805-1430
219-480-4211
www.ivy.tec.in.us/fortwayne

Ivy Tech State College
Northwest Indiana
1440 East Thirty-fifth Avenue
Gary, IN 46409-1479
219-981-1111
www.gar.ivy.tec.in.us

Ivy Tech State College
Central Indiana
One West Twenty-sixth Street
Indianapolis, IN 46208
317-921-4800
www.ivytec.in.us/indianapolis

IOWA

Fire Service Training Bureau
Division of State Fire Marshall
3100 Fire Service Road
Ames, IA 50011-3100
515-294-6817
www.state.ia.us/government/
    dps/fm/fstb

Des Moines Area Community College
2006 Ankeny Boulevard
Ankeny, IA 50021
515-964-6210
www.dmacc.org

Kirkwood Community College
6301 Kirkwood Boulevard SW
PO Box 2068
Cedar Rapids, IA 52406-2068
319-398-5517
www.kirkwood.cc.ia.us

Iowa Western Community College
2700 College Road, Box 4-C
Council Bluffs, IA 51502
712-325-3200
www.iwcc.cc.ia.us

Western Iowa Technical Community College
4647 Stone Avenue
PO Box 5199
Sioux City, IA 51106
712-274-6400
www.witcc.cc.ia.us

KANSAS

Dodge City Community Junior College
2501 North Fourteenth Avenue
Dodge City, KS 67801-2399
316-225-1321
www.dccc.cc.ks.us

Butler County Community College
901 South Haverill Road
El Dorado, KS 67042-3280
316-321-2222
www.buccc.cc.ks.us

Barton County Community College
245 NE Thirtieth Road
Great Bend, KS 67530-9283
316-792-2701
www.barton.cc.ks.us

Hutchinson Community Junior College
1300 North Plum
Hutchinson, KS 67501-5894
316-665-3536
www.hutchcc.edu

Kansas City Kansas Community College
7250 State Avenue
Kansas City, KS 66112-3003
913-334-1100
www.kckcc.cc.kc.us

Johnson County Community College
12345 College Boulevard at Quivira
Overland Park, KS 66210-1299
913-469-8500
www.jccc.ks.net

Labette Community College
200 South Fourteenth
Parsons, KS 67357-4299
316-421-6700
www.labette.cc.ks.us

KENTUCKY

Jefferson Community College

109 East Broadway

Louisville, KY 40202-2005

502-584-0181

www.jcc.uky.edu

Eastern Kentucky University

College of Law Enforcement

Richmond, KY 40475-3101

859-622-2106

www.eku.edu

LOUISIANA

Louisiana State University

Division of Continuing Education

Baton Rouge, LA 70803

225-388-1686

www.lsu.edu

Louisiana State University at Eunice

PO Box 1129

Eunice, LA 70535-1129

337-457-7311

www.lsue.edu

Delgado Community College

615 City Park Avenue

New Orleans, LA 70119-4399

504-671-5012

www.dcc.edu

MAINE

Southern Maine Community College

2 Fort Road

South Portland, ME 04106

207-767-9520

www.smtc.net

MARYLAND

Catonsville Community College

800 South Rolling Road

Catonsville, MD 21228-5381

410-455-4304

www.ccbc.cc.md.us

University of Maryland

Department of Fire Protection Engineering

College Park, MD 20472

301-314-8385

www.uga.umd.edu

Montgomery College

51 Manakee Street

Rockville, MD 20850-1196

301-279-5034

www.montgomerycollege.org

MASSACHUSETTS

Middlesex Community College

591 Springs Road

Bedford, MA 01730-1197

800-818-3434

www.middlesex.cc.ma.us

Bunker Hill Community College
250 New Rutherford Avenue
Boston, MA 02129-2991
617-228-2000
www.bhcc.state.ma.us

Massasoit Community College
290 Thatcher Street
Brockton, MA 02402-3996
508-588-9100
www.massasoit.ma.edu

North Shore Community College
One Ferncroft Road
Danvers, MA 01923-4093
978-762-4000
www.nscc.mass.edu

Northeast Maritime Institute
32 Washington Street
Fairhaven, MA 02719
508-992-4025
www.northeastmaritime.com

Bristol Community College
777 Elsbree Street
Fall River, MA 02720-7395
508-678-2811
www.bristol.mass.edu

Mount Wachusett Community College
444 Green Street
Gardner, MA 01440-1000
978-632-6600 ext. 110
www.mwcc.mass.edu

Greenfield Community College
One College Drive
Greenfield, MA 01301
413-774-3131
www.gcc.mass.edu

Anna Maria College
50 Sunset Lane
Paxton, MA 01612-1198
508-849-3300
www.annamaria.edu

Berkshire Community College
1350 West Street
Pittsfield, MA 01201-5786
413-499-4660
http://cc.berkshire.org

Quincy College
34 Coddington Street
Quincy, MA 02169-4522
617-984-1700
www.quincycollege.com

Salem State College
352 Lafayette Street
Salem, MA 01970
978-542-6000
www.salem.mass.edu

Springfield Technical Community College
One Armory Square
Springfield, MA 01105-1296
413-781-7822
www.stcc.mass.edu

Massachusetts Bay Community College
50 Oakland Street
Wellesley Hills, MA 02481
781-239-3000
www.mbcc.mass.edu

Cape Cod Community College
2240 Iyanough Road
West Barnstable, MA 02668-1599
877-846-3672
www.capecod.mass.edu

Quinsigamond Community College
670 West Boylston Street
Worcester, MA 01606-2092
508-853-2300
www.qcc.mass.edu

Worcester Polytechnic Institute
Center for Fire Safety Studies
100 Institute Road
Worcester, MA 01609-2280
508-831-5286
www.wpi.edu

MICHIGAN

Washtenaw Community College
4800 East Huron River Drive
PO Box D-1
Ann Arbor, MI 48106
734-973-3300
www.washtenaw.cc.mi.us

Oakland Community College
Auburn Hills Campus
2900 Featherstone Road
Auburn Hills, MI 48326-2845
248-232-4100
www.occ.cc.mi.us

Kellogg Community College
450 North Avenue
Battle Creek, MI 49017-3397
616-965-3931
www.kellogg.cc.mi.us

Glen Oaks Community College
62249 Shimmel Road
Centreville, MI 49032-9719
616-467-9945
www.glenoaks.cc.mi.us

Macomb Community College
Center Campus
44575 Garfield Road
Clinton Township, MI 48038-1139
810-286-2228
www.macomb.cc.mi.us

Henry Ford Community College
5101 Evergreen Road
Dearborn, MI 48128
313-845-9600
www.henryford.cc.mi.us

Southwestern Michigan College
58900 Cherry Grove Road
Dowagiac, MI 49047-9793
616-782-1000
www.smc.cc.mi.us

Mott Community College
1401 East Court Street
Flint, MI 48503-2089
810-762-0200
www.program.mcc.edu/fire_protection_
   technology

Mid-Michigan Community College
1375 South Clare Avenue
Harrison, MI 48625-9447
517-386-6622
www.midmich.cc.mi.us

Kalamazoo Valley Community College
PO Box 4070
Kalamazoo, MI 49003-4070
616-372-5000
www.kvcc.edu

Lansing Community College
419 North Capitol Avenue
Lansing, MI 48901-7210
517-483-1957
www.lansing.cc.mi.us

Madonna University
36600 Schoolcraft Road
Livonia, MI 48150-1173
734-432-4951
www.munet.edu

Schoolcraft College
18600 Haggerty Road
Livonia, MI 48152-2696
734-462-4426
www.schoolcraft.cc.mi.us

St. Clair County Community College
323 Erie Street
Port Huron, MI 48061-5015
PO Box 5015
810-989-5500
www.sc4.edu

Lake Superior State University
650 West Easterday Avenue
Sault Ste Marie, MI 49783
906-632-6841
www.lssu.edu

Delta College
Admissions Office
University Center, MI 48710
517-686-9092
www.delta.edu

Macomb Community College
14500 East Twelve Mile Road
Box 309
Warren, MI 48093-3896
866-622-6621
www.macomb.cc.mi.us

MINNESOTA

Lake Superior College
2101 Trinity Road
Duluth, MN 55811
218-733-7600
www.lsc.cc.mn.us

Northwest Technical College
2022 Central Avenue NE
East Grand Forks, MN 56721-2702
218-773-3441
www.ntc-online.com

Hennepin Technical College
13100 College View Drive
Eden Prairie, MN 55347
800-345-4655
www.hennepin.edu

North Hennepin Community College
7411 Eighty-fifth Avenue North
Minneapolis, MN 55445
612-425-3800
www.nh.cc.mn.us

MISSISSIPPI

Mississippi Gulf Coast Community College
Jefferson Davis Campus
2226 Switzer Road
Gulfport, MS 39507
228-896-2500
www.mgccc.cc.ms.us

Meridian Community College
910 Highway 19 North
Meridian, MS 39307
601-484-8622
www.mcc.cc.ms.us

East Mississippi Community College
PO Box 158
Scooba, MS 39358-0158
662-476-8442
www.emcc.cc.ms.us

MISSOURI

University of Missouri
Center for Independent Study
136 Clark Hall
Columbia, MO 65211
573-882-7786
www.missouri.edu

Jefferson College
100 Viking Drive
Hillsboro, MO 63050
636-789-3951
www.jeffco.edu

Penn Valley Community College
3201 Southwest Trafficway
Kansas City, MO 64111
816-759-4101
www.kcmetro.cc.mo.us

Crowder College
601 Laclede Avenue
Neosho, MO 64850-9160
417-451-3223
www.crowder.cc.mo.us

Ozarks Technical Community College
PO Box 5958
Springfield, MO 65801
417-895-7000
www.otc.cc.mo.us

St. Louis Community College
at Florissant Valley
3400 Pershall Road
St. Louis, MO 63135-1499
314-595-4200
www.stlcc.cc.mo.us

St. Louis Community College
at Forest Park
5600 Oakland Avenue
St. Louis, MO 63110-1316
314-644-9100
www.stlcc.cc.mo.us/fp

East Central Missouri Junior College
PO Box 529
Union, MO 63084-0529
636-583-5195
www.ecc.cc.mo.us

University of Central Missouri
School of Public Service
Warrensburg, MO 64093
877-729-8266
www.ucmo.edu

MONTANA

Montana State University
College of Technology–Great Falls
2100 Sixteenth Avenue South
Great Falls, MT 59405
406-771-4312
www.msugs.edu

University of Montana–Helena College of
Technology
1115 North Roberts
Helena, MT 59601
406-444-6800
www.umhelena.edu

Miles Community College
2715 Dickinson Street
Miles City, MT 59301-4799
800-541-9281
www.mcc.cc.mt.us

NEBRASKA

Southeast Community College
Lincoln Campus
8800 O Street
Lincoln, NE 68520-1299
402-471-3333
www.college.sccm.cc.ne.us

University of Nebraska–Lincoln
Office of Admissions
Alexander Building
1410 Q Street
PO Box 880417
Lincoln, NE 68588-0417
402-472-2023
www.unl.edu

Mid-Plains Technical Community College
Interstate 20 and Highway 83
North Platte, NE 69101-9491
308-532-8740
www.mpcc.ne.us

University of Nebraska–Omaha
Alexander Building
College of Engineering
PO Box 688
Omaha, NE 68182
402-554-2800
www.unomaha.edu

NEVADA

Western Nevada Community College
2201 West College Parkway
Carson City, NV 89703
775-445-3000
www.wnc.edu

Great Basin College
1500 College Parkway
Elko, NV 89801
775-738-8493
www.gbcnv.edu

Community College of Southern Nevada
Cheyenne Campus
3200 East Cheyenne Avenue
North Las Vegas, NV 89030-4296
702-651-3038
www.ccsn.nevada.edu

Truckee Meadows Community College
7000 Dandini Boulevard
Reno, NV 89512-3901
775-673-7000
www.tmcc.edu/fireacademy

NEW HAMPSHIRE

New Hampshire Community Technical College
379 New Prescott Hill Road
Laconia, NH 03246
603-524-3207
www.laco.tec.nh.us

NEW JERSEY

Camden County College
PO Box 200
Blackwood, NJ 08012-0200
856-227-7200
www.camdencc.edu

Union County College
1033 Springfield Avenue
Cranford, NJ 07016-1528
908-709-7000
www.ucc.edu

Middlesex County College
2600 Woodbridge Avenue
PO Box 3050
Edison, NJ 08818-3050
732-548-6000
www.middlesex.cc.nj.us

Jersey City State College
2039 Kennedy Boulevard
Jersey City, NJ 07305-1597
201-200-2000
www.jcstate.edu

Brookdale Community College
765 Newman Springs Road
Lincroft, NJ 07738-1597
732-224-2375
www.brookdale.cc.nj.us

Essex County College
303 University Avenue
Newark, NJ 07102-1798
973-877-3000
www.essex.edu

Sussex Community College
One College Hill
Newton, NJ 07860
973-300-2100
www.sussex.cc.nj.us

Passaic County Community College
One College Boulevard
Paterson, NJ 07505-1179
973-684-6868
www.pccc.cc.nj.us

Burlington County College
County Road 530
Pemberton, NJ 08068-1599
609-894-4900
www.bcc.edu

Ocean County College
College Drive
PO Box 2001
Toms River, NJ 08754-2001
732-255-0400
www.ocean.cc.nj.us

Mercer County Community College
West Windsor Campus
1200 Old Trenton Road
Trenton, NJ 08690-1004
609-586-4800
www.mccc.edu

Thomas Edison State College
101 West State Street
Trenton, NJ 08608-1176
609-292-6565
www.tesc.edu

Essex County College, West Essex Campus
730 Bloomfield Avenue
West Caldwell, NJ 07006
201-403-2560
www.essex.edu

NEW MEXICO

New Mexico State University at Alamogordo
PO Box 477
2400 North Scenic Drive
Alamogordo, NM 88310
505-439-3600
http://alamo.nmsu.edu

Albuquerque Technical Vocational Institute
525 Buena Vista Southeast
Albuquerque, NM 87106-4096
505-224-3000
www.tvi.cc.nm.us

New Mexico State University–Carlsbad
1500 University Drive
Carlsbad, NM 88220-3509
505-234-9200
http://cavern.nmsu.edu

Clovis Community College
417 Schepps Boulevard
Clovis, NM 88101-8381
505-769-2811
www.clovis.cc.nm.us

New Mexico Junior College
5317 Lovington Highway
Hobbs, NM 88240-9123
800-657-6260
www.nmjc.cc.nm.us

Dona Ana Branch Community College
MSC 3DA, PO Box 30001
New Mexico State University
Las Cruces, NM 88003-8001
505-527-7647
http://dabcc-www.nmsu.edu

Eastern New Mexico University–Roswell
PO Box 6000
Roswell, NM 88201
505-624-7000
www.roswell.enmu.edu

NEW YORK

Broome Community College
Upper Front Street
PO Box 1017
Binghamton, NY 13902-1017
607-778-5000
www.sunybroome.edu

Corning Community College
One Academic Drive
Corning, NY 14830-3297
607-962-9220
www.corning-cc.edu

Mercy College
555 Broadway
Dobbs Ferry, NY 10522-1189
800-MERCY-NY (800-637-2969)
www.mercynet.edu

John Jay College of Criminal Justice/CUNY
Fire Science Division, Room 3529N
899 Tenth Avenue
New York, NY 10019
212-237-8000
www.jjay.cuny.edu

Erie Community College, South Campus
4041 Southwestern Boulevard
Orchard Park, NY 14127-2199
716-851-1003
www.ecc.edu

Monroe Community College
1000 East Henrietta Road
PO Box 9720
Rochester, NY 14623-5780
716-292-2000
www.monroecc.edu

Schenectady County Community College
78 Washington Avenue
Schenectady, NY 12305-2294
518-381-1366
www.sunysccc.edu

Rockland Community College
145 College Road
Suffern, NY 10901-3699
914-574-4237
www.sunyrockland.edu

Onondaga Community College
4941 Onondaga Road
Syracuse, NY 13215
315-469-2201
www.sunyocc.edu

NORTH CAROLINA

Central Piedmont Community College
PO Box 35009
Charlotte, NC 28235-5009
704-330-2722
www.cpcc.cc.nc.us

Gaston College
201 Highway 321 South
Dallas, NC 28034
704-922-6214
www.gastoncollege.org

Durham Technical Community College
1637 Lawson Street
Durham, NC 27703-5023
919-686-3300
www.dtcc.cc.nc.us

Alamance Community College
PO Box 8000
Graham, NC 27253
336-578-2002
www.alamance.cc.nc.us

Coastal Carolina Community College
444 Western Boulevard
Jacksonville, NC 28546-6877
910-455-1221
www.coastalcarolina.org

Guilford Technical Community College
PO Box 309
Jamestown, NC 27282-0309
336-334-4822, ext. 5350
www.technet.gtcc.cc.nc.us

Lenoir Community College
PO Box 188
Kinston, NC 28502-0188
252-527-6223
www.lenoir.cc.nc.us

Davidson County Community College
PO Box 1287
Lexington, NC 27293-1287
336-249-8186
www.davidson.cc.nc.us

Cape Fear Community College
411 North Front Street
Wilmington, NC 28401
910-251-5100
www.cfcc.net

Wilson Technical Community College
PO Box 4305
Wilson, NC 27893-3310
252-291-1195
www.wilsontech.cc.nc.us

NORTH DAKOTA

North Dakota State University
1301 Twelfth Avenue North
Fargo, ND 58105
701-231-8011
www.nsu.nodak.edu/forestservice/fire/
    wildfire_training.htm

OHIO

University of Akron
302 East Buchtel Mall
Akron, OH 44325-2001
330-972-7100
www.uakron.edu

Bowling Green State University
Continuing Education Division
40 College Park
Bowling Green, OH 43403-0001
419-372-2531
www.bgsu.edu

Stark Technical College
6200 Frank Avenue NW
Canton, OH 44720-7299
330-966-5450
www.stark.cc.oh.us

University of Cincinnati
College of Applied Science
100 East Central Park
Cincinnati, OH 45216
513-556-1100
www.uc.edu

Cuyahoga Community College
Metropolitan Campus
2900 Community College Avenue
Cleveland, OH 44115
216-987-4030
www.tri-c.cc.oh.us

Sinclair Community College
444 West Third Street
Dayton, OH 45402-1460
937-512-2500
www.sinclair.edu

Delaware Area Career Center
1610 State Route 521
Delaware, OH 43015-9001
740-363-1993
www.delawareareacc.org

Lorain County Community College
1005 Abbe Road North
Elyria, OH 44035-1691
800-995-LCCC
www.lorainccc.edu

Lakeland Community College
7700 Clocktower Drive
Kirtland, OH 44094-5198
440-953-7000
www.lakeland.cc.oh.us

Hocking College
3301 Hocking Parkway
Nelsonville, OH 45764-9588
740-753-3591
www.hocking.edu

Cuyahoga Community College
Western Campus
11000 Pleasant Valley Road
Parma, OH 44130-5199
216-987-5000
www.tri-ccc.oh.us

Owens Community College–Toledo
PO Box 10000
Oregon Road
Toledo, OH 43699-1947
800-GO-OWENS (800-466-9367)
www.owens.cc.oh.us

OKLAHOMA

Oklahoma State University
Technical Institute
900 North Portland Avenue
Oklahoma City, OK 73107-6120
405-945-3270
www.okstate.edu

Oklahoma State University
219 Student Union
Stillwater, OK 74078
405-744-5358
http://osu.okstate.edu

Tulsa Junior College
7505 West Forty-first Street
Tulsa, OK 74107
918-595-7000
www.tulsa.cc.ok.us

OREGON

Clatsop Community College
1653 Jerome Avenue
Astoria, OR 97103-3698
503-325-0910
www.clatsopcollege.com

Central Oregon Community College
2600 Northwest College Way
Bend, OR 97701-5998
503-383-7500
www.cocc.edu

Southwestern Oregon Community College
1988 Newmark Avenue
Coos Bay, OR 97420-2912
800-962-2838
www.southwestern.cc.or.us

Lane Community College
4000 East Thirtieth Avenue
Eugene, OR 97405
541-747-4501
http://lanecc.edu

Rogue Community College
Redwood Campus
3345 Redwood Highway
Grants Pass, OR 97527-9298
541-956-7500
www.rogue.cc.or.us

Mt. Hood Community College
2600 SE Stark
Gresham, OR 97030-3300
503-491-6422
www.mhcc.cc.or.us

Eastern Oregon State College
One University Boulevard
Division of Distance Education
La Grande, OR 97850-2899
541-962-3672
www.eosc.osshe.edu

Western Oregon State College
345 North Monmouth Avenue
Monmouth, OR 97361
877-877-1593
www.wou.edu

Portland Community College
1200 SW Foty-ninth Avenue
Portland, OR 97280-0990
503-977-4621
www.pcc.edu

Umpqua Community College
1140 College Road
Roseburg, OR 97470
541-440-4600
www.umpqua.cc.or.us

Chemeketa Community College
4000 Lancaster Drive NE
Salem, OR 97309-7070
503-399-5000
www.chemek.cc.or.us

PENNSYLVANIA

Montgomery County Community College
340 Dekalb Pike
Blue Bell, PA 19422-0796
215-641-6300
www.mc3.edu

Harrisburg Area Community College
One HACC Drive
Harrisburg, PA 17110-2999
717-780-2300
www.hacc.edu

Delaware County Community College
901 South Media Line Road
Media, PA 19063-1094
610-359-5050
www.dccc.edu

Community College of Allegheny County
Boyce Campus
595 Beatty Road
Monroeville, PA 15146-1396
724-325-6614
www.ccac.edu

Luzerne County Community College
1333 South Prospect Street
Nanticoke, PA 18634-3899
800-377-LCCC (800-377-5222)
www.luzerne.edu

Community College of Philadelphia
1700 Spring Garden Street
Philadelphia, PA 19130-3991
215-751-8000
www.ccp.cc.pa.us

Community College of Allegheny County
South Campus
1750 Clairton Road
West Mifflin, PA 15122-3097
412-469-4301
www.ccac.edu

Westmoreland County Community College
400 Armbrust Road
Youngwood, PA 15697
724-925-4000
www.westmoreland.cc.pa.us

RHODE ISLAND

Providence College
School of Continuing Education
Providence, RI 02918
401-865-1000
www.providence.edu

Community College of Rhode Island
Knight Campus
400 East Avenue
Warwick, RI 02886-1807
401-825-1000
www.ccri.edu

SOUTH CAROLINA

Greenville Technical College
PO Box 5616
Greenville, SC 29606-5616
803-250-8111
www.greenvilletech.com

Midlands Technical College
Airport Campus
1260 Lexington Drive
West Columbia, SC 29170
803-738-8324
-or-
800-922-8038
www.mid.tec.sc.us

SOUTH DAKOTA

Kilian Community College
224 North Phillips Avenue
Sioux Falls, SD 57104-6014
605-336-1711
http://kcc.cc.sd.us

TENNESSEE

Chattanooga State Technical Community
College
4501 Amnicola Highway
Chattanooga, TN 37406-1018
423-697-4400
www.cstcc.cc.tn.us

Volunteer State Community College
1480 Nashville Pike
Gallatin, TN 37066
615-230-3688
-or-
888-335-8722
www.vscc.cc.tn.us

Roane State Community College
276 Patton Lane
Harriman, TN 37748
865-882-4523
-or-
800-345-9104
www.rscc.cc.tn.us

Southwest Tennesee Community College
5983 Macon Cove
Memphis, TN 38134
888-TECH-YES (888-832-4937)
-or-
901-382-TECH (901-382-8324)
-or-
901-333-4111
www.stcc.cc.tn.us

University of Memphis
Memphis, TN 38152
901-678-2111
www.memphis.edu

Tennessee Technology Center
at Murfreesboro
1303 Old Fort Parkway
Murfreesboro, TN 37130
615-898-8010
www.murfreesboro.tec.tn.us

TEXAS

Cisco Junior College
841 North Judge Ely Blvd.
Abilene, TX 79601
915-673-4567
www.cisco.cc.tx.us

Amarillo College
PO Box 447
Amarillo, TX 79178-0001
806-371-5030
www.uctx.edu

Trinity Valley Community College
100 Cardinal Drive
Athens, TX 75751
903-677-TVCC (903-677-8822)
www.tvcc.cc.tx.us

Austin Community College
1212 Rio Grande
Austin, TX 78701
512-223-3030
www.austin.cc.tx.us

Lamar Institute of Technology
PO Box 10043
Beaumont, TX 77710
409-880-8185
http://theinstitute.lamar.edu

The University of Texas at Brownsville and
Texas Southmost College
80 Fort Brown Street
Brownsville, TX 78520
956-544-8200
www.utb.edu

Blinn College, Bryan Campus
PO Box 6030
Bryan, TX 77805-6030
979-821-0220
www.blinncol.edu

Texas Engineering Extension Service
Emergency Services Training Institute
John B. Connolly Building
301 Tarrow, TEEX
College Station, TX 77840-7896
http://teexweb.tamu.edu

Del Mar College
101 Baldwin Boulevard
Corpus Christi, TX 78404-3897
361-698-1255
-or-
800-652-3357
www.delmar.edu

Navarro College
3200 West Seventh Avenue
Corsicana, TX 75110
903-874-6501
-or-
800-NAVARRO (800-628-2776)
www.nav.cc.tx.us

El Paso Community College
PO Box 20500
El Paso, TX 79998-0500
915-831-2000
www.epcc.edu

Fort Worth Fire Training Academy
1000 Calvert Street
Fort Worth, TX 76107
817-871-6875
www.fwfd.net

Tarrant County College
Mary Owen Center
1500 Houston Street
Fort Worth, TX 76102-6599
817-515-5100
www.tcjc.cc.tx.us

Houston Community College
4310 Dunlaby
Houston, TX 77006
713-718-6111
www.hccs.cc.tx.us

Kilgore College Fire Academy
100 Broadway
Kilgore, TX 75662
903-984-8662
www.kilgore.cc.tx.us

Laredo Community College
West End Washington Street
Laredo, TX 78040-4395
210-721-5108
www.laredo.cc.tx.us

South Plains College
1401 South College Avenue
Levelland, TX 79336
806-894-9611
www.spc.cc.tx.us

Collin County Community College
Central Park Campus
2200 West University Drive
PO Box 8001
McKinney, TX 75070
972-548-6790
www.ccccd.edu

Midland College
3600 North Garfield
Midland, TX 79705-6399
915-685-4500
www.midland.cc.tx.us

Odessa College
201 West University
Odessa, TX 79764-7127
915-335-6432
www.odessa.edu

San Jacinto College
Central Campus
PO Box 2007
8060 Spencer Highway
Pasadena, TX 77501-2007
281-476-1501
www.sjcd.cc.tx.us

San Antonio College
1300 San Pedro Avenue
San Antonio, TX 78212
210-733-2000
www.accd.edu

Tyler Junior College
PO Box 9020
Tyler, TX 75711-9020
903-510-2238
www.tyler.cc.tx.us

UTAH
Utah Valley State College/Utah Fire and
Rescue Academy
3131 Mike Jense Parkway
Provo, UT 84601
801-764-7700
www.uvsc.edu/ufra

VERMONT
Southeastern Vermont Career Education
Center (technical high school)
50 Fairground Road
Brattleboro, VT 05301
802-257-7335
www.svcec.org

VIRGINIA
Northern Virginia Community College
8333 Little River Turnpike
Annandale, VA 22003-3796
703-323-3400
www.nv.cc.va.us

Thomas Nelson Community College
PO Box 9407
Hampton, VA 23670
757-825-2700
www.tncc.cc.va.us

J. Sargeant Reynolds Community College
108 East Grace Street
PO Box 85622
Richmond, VA 23285-5622
804-371-3029
www.jsr.cc.va.us

Tidewater Community College
Virginia Beach Campus
1700 College Crescent
Virginia Beach, VA 23456
757-822-7255
www.tc.cc.va.us

WASHINGTON

Bellevue Community College
3000 Landerholm Circle SE
Bellevue, WA 98007-6484
206-641-2222
www.bcc.ctc.edu

Olympic College
1600 Chester Avenue
Bremerton, WA 98337-1699
360-475-7723
http://oc.ctc.edu

Lower Columbia College
1600 Maple
PO Box 3010
Longview, WA 98632-0310
360-577-2311
http://lcc.ctc.edu

Edmonds Community College
20000 Sixty-eighth Avenue West
Lynnwood, WA 98036-5999
425-640-1459
www.edcc.edu

South Puget Sound Community College
2011 Moltman Road SW
Olympia, WA 98512
360-754-7711
www.spscc.ctc.edu

Columbia Basin Community College
2600 North Twentieth Avenue
Pasco, WA 99301
509-547-0511
www.cbc2.org

Spokane Community College
1810 North Greene Street
Spokane, WA 99207-5399
509-533-7000
www.scc.spokane.cc.wa.us

Bates Technical College
1101 South Yakima Avenue
Tacoma, WA 98405-4895
253-680-7000
www.bates.ctc.edu

Pierce College at Fort Steilacoom
9401 Farwest Drive SW
Tacoma, WA 98498
253-964-6500
www.pierce.ctc.edu

Wenatchee Valley College
1300 Fifth Street
Wenatchee, WA 98801
509-662-1651
www.wvc.ctc.edu

Yakima Valley Community College
PO Box 22520
Yakima, WA 98907-2520
509-574-4600
www.yvcc.cc.wa.us

WEST VIRGINIA

Shepherd College
PO Box 3210
Shepherdstown, WV 25443-3210
304-876-5000
www.shepherd.wvnet.edu

WISCONSIN

Fox Valley Technical College
1825 North Bluemound Drive
PO Box 2277
Appleton, WI 54912-2277
920-735-5600
www.foxvalley.tec.wi.us

Lakeshore Technical College
1290 North Avenue
Cleveland, WI 53015
888-468-6582
www.gotoltc.com

Chippewa Valley Technical College
620 West Clairemont Avenue
Eau Claire, WI 54701
715-833-6200
-or-
800-547-2882
www.chippewa.tec.wi.us

Moraine Park Technical College
PO Box 1940
235 North National Avenue
Fond du Lac, WI 54935-1940
414-922-8611
www.moraine.tec.wi.us

Northeast Wisconsin Technical College
2740 West Mason Street
Green Bay, WI 53407-9042
715-735-9361
-or-
800-422-NWTC (800-422-6982)
www.nwtconline.com

Blackhawk Technical College
6004 Prairie Road
PO Box 5009
Janesville, WI 53547
608-757-7713
www.blackhawk.tec.wi.us

Madison Area Technical College
3550 Anderson Street
Madison, WI 53704
608-246-6100
-or-
800-322-6282
www.madison.tec.wi.us

Wisconsin Indianhead Technical College
1019 South Knowles Avenue
New Richmond, WI 54017
715-246-6561
-or-
800-243-9482
www.witc.edu

Milwaukee Area Technical College
South Campus
6665 South Howell Avenue
Oak Creek, WI 53154-1196
414-571-4500
www.milwaukee.tec.wi.us

Gateway Technical College
1001 South Main Street
Racine, WI 53403
262-619-6232
www.gateway.tec.wi.us

Mid-State Technical College
500 Thirty-second Street North
Wisconsin Rapids, WI 54494
715-422-5300
www.midstate.tec.wi.us

WYOMING

Casper College
125 College Drive
Casper, WY 82601
307-268-2110
www.cc.whecn.edu

Laramie County Community College
1400 East College Drive
Cheyenne, WY 82007
307-778-LCCC (307-778-5222)
www.lcc.whecn.edu

Participating Colleges and Universities: Degrees at a Distance (Open Learning Fire Service Program)

Cogswell Polytechnical College
1175 Bordeaux Drive
Sunnyvale, CA 94089
800-264-7955
E-mail: info@cogswell.edu
www.cogswell.edu
States served: AZ, CA, NV

State University of New York (SUNY)
Empire State College
Center for Distance Learning
111 West Avenue
Saratoga Springs, NY 12866
518-587-2100, ext. 315
Fax: 518-587-2660
E-mail: cdl@esc.edu
www.esc.edu
States served: CT, ME, MA, NH, NY, PA, RI, VT

University of Cincinnati
College of Applied Science
2220 Victory Parkway
Cincinnati, OH 45206
513-556-6567
Fax: 513-556-5056
www.uc.edu/colleges/cas
States served: FL, GA, IN, MI, MN, ND, OH,
    SD, WI

University of Maryland
University College
Undergraduate Programs
3501 University Boulevard
Hyattsville, MD 20783
800-283-6832
www.universities.com/Distance_Learning/
University_of_Maryland_University_College
.html
States served: DE, MD, NJ, NC, DC,
    WV, VA

University of Memphis
University College
218 Brister Hall
Memphis, TN 38152-6150
901-678-2716
Fax: 901-678-4913
www.uc.memphis.edu
States served: AL, AR, KY, LA, MS, SC, TN

Western Illinois University
Nontraditional Programs
Honaburn Hall 6
Macomb, Illinois 61445
309-298-1929
Fax: 309-298-2154
E-mail: distancelearning@wiu.edu
www.wiu.edu
States served: IL, IA, KS, MO, NE, NM,
    OK, TX

Western Oregon University
Division of Extended Programs
345 North Monmouth Avenue
Monmouth, OR 97361
800-451-5767
E-mail: extend@wou.edu
www.wou.edu
States served: AK, CO, HI, ID, MT, OR, UT,
    WA, WY